The Autonomous Analyst

Leveraging LLMs and Transformers for Market Insight

Victor Trex

Published by NobleTrex Press

For permissions and other inquiries, write to:
P.O. Box 3132, Framingham, MA 01701, USA

Contents

1 **Market and Data Foundations for Autonomous Analysis** **5**

1.1 Asset Classes, Participants, and Microstructure 5

1.2 Corporate Disclosures, News, and Alternative Data . . 18

1.3 Time Series Characteristics and Market Regimes 32

2 **Quantitative and ML Foundations** **47**

2.1 Probability, Statistics, and Uncertainty Quantification . 47

2.2 Linear Algebra, Calculus, and Optimization for Modeling 62

2.3 Supervised Learning and Classical Time-Series Models 75

3 **Transformer and LLM Fundamentals** **89**

3.1 Tokenization, Embeddings, and Semantic Similarity . . 89

3.2 Attention Mechanics and Transformer Architecture . . 102

3.3 Pretraining, Fine-Tuning, and Long-Context Modeling 114

4 **Data Engineering for Retrieval-Augmented Finance** **127**

4.1 Ingestion, Quality, and Lineage Pipelines 127

4.2 Feature Engineering and Vectorized Knowledge Graphs 140

4.3 Streaming and Real-Time Data Infrastructure 153

5 LLM System Design and Agentic Workflows 167

5.1 Prompt Engineering and Function Calling 167

5.2 Retrieval-Augmented Generation and Temporal Retrieval178

5.3 Structured Extraction and Agent Orchestration 189

6 Quant Applications and Portfolio Execution 201

6.1 Sentiment, News, and Event-Driven Signals 201

6.2 Filings Analysis and Signal Fusion with Time Series . . 214

6.3 Portfolio Construction, Execution, and Impact Modeling 227

7 Evaluation, Backtesting, and Operational Governance237

7.1 Leakage Control, Benchmarks, and Backtesting Discipline237

7.2 Risk Management, Causal Inference, and Multiple Testing251

7.3 Serving, Monitoring, and Compliance in Production . . 262

Introduction

Markets have always been narratives written in numbers, but in recent years the text itself has become a first-class signal: filings, earnings calls, social discourse, alt-data exhaust, and the machine logs of electronic microstructure. Large language models (LLMs) and transformers offer a way to read this deluge at scale, connect it to structured fundamentals, and act-carefully-under uncertainty. This book is about designing an "autonomous analyst": a system that can ingest heterogeneous data, reason with financial and statistical discipline, invoke tools, and produce auditable outputs that a portfolio can trust.

By autonomy we do not mean an unbounded, self-directed trader. We mean a model-augmented workflow that is grounded in retrieval, explicit about timing, aligned with risk and compliance constraints, and engineered for reproducibility. The system should cite what it reads, respect market microstructure and transaction costs, and make its assumptions legible. It should propose actions with quantified uncertainty, and it should fail safely-preferring to defer, ask for more data, or escalate to a human when signals are ambiguous.

Our approach is deliberately integrative. Transformers alone do not yield alpha; they sit inside a broader stack that spans market knowledge, statistical inference, data engineering, and execution. The book therefore weaves together six threads: market foundations; quantitative and ML basics; transformer mechanics; retrieval-augmented data systems; agentic LLM workflows; and the translation of model outputs into portfolio decisions. Throughout, we emphasize time: point-in-time correctness, regime shifts, walk-forward evaluation, and the difference between correlation and causation when text meets price.

Chapter 1, Market and Data Foundations for Autonomous Analysis, situates the work in actual trading conditions. We examine asset classes, venues, and order-to-execution pathways; then survey corporate disclosures, news, and alternative data with an eye to timeliness, conventions, and ingestion constraints. We close by reviewing time-series properties-stationarity, volatility clustering, and regime changes-that shape any downstream modeling and evaluation.

Chapter 2, Quantitative and ML Foundations, builds the toolkit for thinking clearly about uncertainty and model behavior. The discussion moves from probability and inference to the linear algebra and optimization used in modern training loops, and then to supervised learning and classical time-series baselines. The goal is not encyclopedic coverage, but enough rigor to diagnose leakage, construct defensible benchmarks, and understand why a given model is likely to generalize-or fail.

Chapter 3, Transformer and LLM Fundamentals, explains how tokens become embeddings, how attention composes information, and how pretraining objectives induce capabilities. We detail fine-tuning strategies, alignment considerations, and long-context techniques essential for reading filings and earnings transcripts. The emphasis is on constraints as much as capabilities: throughput, latency, and the tradeoffs that matter in production.

Chapter 4, Data Engineering for Retrieval-Augmented Finance, turns to the pipelines that make LLMs useful. We design ingestion and quality contracts with lineage, build features and vector knowledge graphs that marry entities across text and tables, and outline streaming infrastructure for real-time analytics. The outcome is a traceable, point-in-time store that models can query to ground their claims.

Chapter 5, LLM System Design and Agentic Workflows, synthesizes prompting, retrieval, function calling, and orchestration. We show how agents decompose financial tasks-retrieve, extract, validate, summarize-while managing memory, retries, and guardrails. Time-aware retrieval and structured outputs are treated as first-class citizens so that downstream consumers, human or automated, can trust and audit the chain of reasoning.

Chapter 6, Quant Applications and Portfolio Execution, connects signals to P&L. We build event-driven and sentiment-aware predictors, extract KPIs from filings, and fuse text with numerical series. We then face market reality: portfolio construction under risk budgets, turnover and capacity constraints, and execution with impact modeling. The chapter's throughline is translation-turning model statements into trades that survive costs and slippage.

The book closes with Evaluation, Backtesting, and Operational Governance. Here we codify leakage controls, temporal splits, and walk-forward discipline; address risk management, causal identification, and multiple testing; and detail serving, monitoring, privacy, and model-risk management in regulated environments. Autonomous does not mean unsupervised: credibility, safety, and compliance are features, not afterthoughts.

Who is this book for? Practitioners building research or production systems, quants incorporating unstructured data, data engineers and MLOps teams in financial contexts, and students seeking a coherent path from transformer fundamentals to tradable insight. A working knowledge of Python, basic statistics, and financial vocabulary is helpful but not strictly required; each chapter motivates the necessary concepts and points to deeper references.

Finally, a word on scope and stance. We are pragmatic idealists: enthusiastic about what LLMs can do when grounded in data that is clean, time-aware, and auditable; conservative about claims that outrun evidence. The autonomous analyst we describe is a partner to human judgment, not a replacement-augmenting attention, compressing latency from event to decision, and making the research ledger legible end to end.

Chapter 1

Market and Data Foundations for Autonomous Analysis

Autonomous analysts do not live in the abstract-they reason about real orders, real disclosures, and real price paths. Before we hand markets to transformers, we need to understand the world those models are supposed to explain: who trades with whom, on which venues, under which rules; how information flows through filings, news, and alternative data streams; and why time series of prices refuse to behave like tidy textbook examples. This chapter builds that foundation, giving you a concrete mental model of market plumbing and data-generating processes so that subsequent modeling and LLM orchestration rest on solid empirical ground rather than convenient myths.

1.1 Asset Classes, Participants, and Microstructure

In the previous chapter we treated prices and returns largely as abstract time series. For an autonomous analyst, that abstraction is not enough.

A learning system that interprets every price update as if it were a clean, continuous signal will systematically misread markets that are actually discrete, strategic, and full of frictions.

This section moves one level closer to the trading floor. We begin with *what* is traded (asset classes), then discuss *who* trades (market participants and their objectives), and finally examine *how* trading actually happens at the microstructural level (order books, venues, and tick-by-tick data). The goal is to connect each row in a trades or quotes file to the economic and strategic forces that produced it.

A Practical Taxonomy of Asset Classes

From an autonomous analyst's perspective, the most important question about an instrument is: *what exactly changes hands when a trade occurs, and what economic exposure does that create?* The standard asset-class labels are a convenient starting point.

Equities

What is traded. In listed equities, the traded object is typically a share of common stock. One share is a unit of ownership in a firm. There may also be different share classes (e.g., voting vs. non-voting), but at the data level each symbol (ticker) represents a specific instrument.

Economic exposure. Holding a share entitles the investor to:

- A residual claim on the firm's cash flows (after debt and other obligations).
- Potential dividends and buybacks.
- Voting rights (for most common stock).

For an LLM-based analyst, equities have several features that matter for data ingestion and modeling:

- *Firm-specific mapping:* Each ticker corresponds to a legal entity with rich textual context (filings, news, product descriptions).

- *Corporate events:* Splits, dividends, mergers, and ticker changes alter the price and return series in ways that must be adjusted before training.
- *High microstructural richness:* Equities are heavily traded on limit order books, providing deep tick-level data.

Fixed Income

What is traded. In fixed income markets (government bonds, corporate bonds, securitized products), the traded instrument is a claim on future cash flows usually defined by:

- A face (par) value.
- A coupon rate and schedule, or a floating-rate formula.
- A maturity date and repayment mechanism.

Some bonds trade on exchanges, but many trade over-the-counter (OTC) via dealers, leading to less transparent and sparser tick data.

Economic exposure. A bond position exposes the holder to:

- Interest-rate risk (changes in the yield curve).
- Credit risk (probability of default and recovery value).
- Liquidity risk (ability to unwind at reasonable cost).

For autonomous analysis, bond data often appears as:

- *Quotes and trades* reported with delay or only above certain size thresholds.
- *Derived yields and spreads* (e.g., spread to government curve).

Models must therefore cope with irregular sampling and missing observations.

Foreign Exchange (FX)

What is traded. In FX, the traded object is a *currency pair*, such as EUR/USD. A single transaction exchanges one currency for another at a negotiated or quoted rate. Markets are largely OTC but highly electronic.

Economic exposure. A position in EUR/USD reflects the relative value and monetary conditions of two economies. FX is central to:

- Global macro strategies and cross-border investing.
- Hedging of foreign revenues and costs.

FX microstructure has specific traits:

- Very high liquidity and tight spreads in major pairs.
- A network of interdealer platforms and single-dealer portals.
- Streaming quotes that resemble exchange order books, but with more bilateral customization.

Listed Derivatives

What is traded. On futures and options exchanges, participants trade standardized *contracts*. A futures contract references an underlying asset (e.g., equity index, bond, commodity, crypto) and specifies standardized terms: contract size, delivery month, tick size, and so on. Options add strike prices and exercise style.

Economic exposure. Derivatives provide:

- Leverage and convexity (especially options).
- Exposure to volatility, basis (futures vs. spot), and term structure.

From a data perspective, derivatives multiply the number of tradable instruments:

- Many contracts per underlying (across expiries and strikes).
- Complex relationships (e.g., put–call parity, calendar spreads) that link prices.

Autonomous systems must track contract specifications carefully; naïvely stacking nearby contracts into a single time series can introduce jumps and artifacts.

Digital Assets

Lastly, digital assets such as cryptocurrencies and tokens exhibit both familiar and novel features:

- **What is traded:** Units on a blockchain ledger (e.g., BTC, ETH), or tokens representing governance, utilities, or claims on protocols.
- **Venues:** Centralized exchanges and decentralized exchanges (DEXs) running on-chain.
- **Unique data:** On-chain transaction graphs, smart contract events, and protocol-level metrics.

For an LLM-based system, digital assets are interesting because the boundary between *market data* and *fundamental data* blurs: some fundamentals are transparently encoded in code and on-chain behavior.

Who Trades: Participant Types and Objectives

Prices and volumes emerge from the interaction of heterogeneous agents. To interpret tick-level data, a model should have at least a coarse mental model of who is on each side of the trade and why.

Retail Investors

Retail investors are individual traders using brokerage platforms or apps. Their trades are often:

- Small in size relative to institutional blocks.
- Event-driven (earnings, news) or sentiment-driven.
- Constrained by margin rules and limited leverage.

Retail flow can be informative (e.g., when crowds rapidly coordinate around news) or noisy. Some venues and intermediaries monetize retail order flow by internalizing it or routing it to wholesalers.

Asset Managers

Long-only mutual funds, pension funds, and insurance companies fall into this category. Their main characteristics:

- **Objectives:** Meet benchmark-relative or absolute-return mandates over medium to long horizons.
- **Constraints:** Regulatory limits, investment guidelines, and often low turnover.
- **Execution style:** Large orders sliced over time to reduce impact; heavy use of algorithms and crossing networks.

In tick data, their footprints may appear as persistent buying or selling pressure over hours or days, often at times of higher liquidity (e.g., near the open or close).

Hedge Funds and Prop Trading Firms

These are active managers with more flexible mandates and, often, higher leverage:

- **Objectives:** Absolute returns, alpha generation, arbitrage.
- **Strategies:** From long-term fundamental to short-term statistical arbitrage and high-frequency trading (HFT).
- **Execution:** Sophisticated algorithms, co-location, and custom infrastructure.

At high frequencies, many of the quotes and cancellations in a limit order book originate from such entities.

Dealers and Market Makers

Dealers and designated market makers (DMMs) supply liquidity by continuously quoting bid and ask prices:

- **Compensation:** They earn the spread and sometimes rebates from exchanges.

- **Risk:** They must manage inventory risk and adverse selection (being hit when they are wrong).
- **Behavior in data:** Frequent quote updates, depth provision on both sides, and fast pullbacks during volatility spikes.

An autonomous analyst must recognize that spreads, depths, and short-term price dynamics are heavily shaped by liquidity providers' risk constraints.

Issuers and Corporates

Firms themselves interact with markets via:

- Primary issuance (IPOs, bond offerings).
- Secondary actions (buybacks, stock-based compensation, tender offers).
- Hedging programs (FX, commodities, interest rates).

These flows can be large and strategic, often executed via dealers. They are less visible in raw tick data but important in understanding medium-horizon supply and demand.

A Layered View: Assets, Participants, and the Order Book

We can now connect *what* is traded and *who* trades it to the *mechanism* that turns orders into trades.

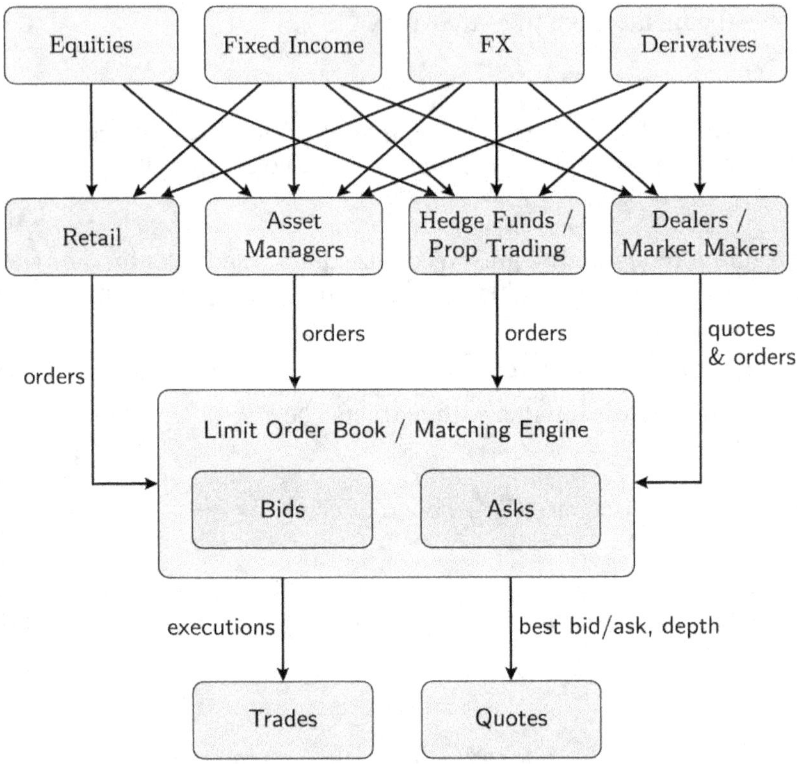

This layered picture emphasizes that the tick-by-tick feed you hand to an LLM agent is the *output* of a process where heterogeneous participants route orders in different asset classes to matching engines that enforce market rules.

Microstructure Basics: Orders, Quotes, and Trades

At the core of modern electronic markets is the *limit order book* (LOB). Understanding its mechanics is essential for interpreting tick data.

Order Types

The simplest order types are:

Limit order. A limit order specifies:

- a side (buy or sell),
- a price limit,
- and a quantity.

A buy limit order at price p says: "Buy up to this quantity, but never pay more than p." A sell limit order at p says: "Sell up to this quantity, but never accept less than p." If a limit order cannot be fully matched immediately, the unmatched portion rests in the order book.

Market order. A market order specifies only side and quantity. It says: "Execute this quantity immediately at the best available prices." Market orders cross the spread and consume liquidity provided by resting limit orders.

Real-world venues support many variations (stop orders, pegged orders, hidden and iceberg orders), but they can usually be understood as combinations or modifications of these two primitives.

From Orders to the Order Book

The limit order book is a sorted list of all active buy and sell limit orders:

- On the *bid side*, buy orders are stacked from highest price (best bid) downwards.
- On the *ask side*, sell orders are stacked from lowest price (best ask) upwards.

When a new order arrives:

- If it is a market order, or a limit order whose price is *aggressive* enough to hit existing orders on the other side, a trade occurs at the previously resting order's price.
- Any remaining unfilled portion may either rest (if it is a limit order that is not fully aggressive) or be canceled (e.g., if the order is market-type or has fill-or-kill conditions).

This sequence of events produces three key data streams:

- **Order messages:** submissions, modifications, and cancellations.
- **Quotes:** snapshots of the best bid/ask and depth at each price level.
- **Trades:** executed transactions, including price, size, and time.

Most downstream analysis works with quotes and trades; some specialized strategies use full order-message feeds.

Bid–Ask Spread, Depth, and Liquidity

The *bid–ask spread* is the difference between the best ask and best bid prices. It represents the cost of executing a round-trip trade (buy then sell) at the prevailing quotes, before fees.

- A narrow spread usually indicates intense competition among liquidity providers and high liquidity.
- A wide spread can signal low liquidity, high uncertainty, or both.

Depth at a price level is the total quantity available at that price. The *order book depth profile* across multiple levels reflects how much size can be traded before the price moves.

For an autonomous analyst, these microstructural measures are key features:

- Short-horizon strategies may use them directly as inputs (e.g., "predict the next 100 ms price move given current depth").
- Longer-horizon systems still need to understand that not all prices are equally easy to transact at; liquidity risk matters.

Venues, Routing, and Dark Liquidity

Modern markets are fragmented across many trading venues. A single stock may trade on multiple exchanges and off-exchange facilities.

Lit Exchanges

Lit exchanges publish their order books (or at least best bid and ask) in real time. They:

- Accept and match orders according to transparent rules.
- Publish trades and quotes that feed into consolidated tapes.

Most tick-level datasets that analysts work with are consolidated feeds from lit exchanges.

Dark Pools and Internalizers

Dark venues differ in that they do not display full pre-trade information:

- **Dark pools** match buy and sell interest at reference prices (often derived from lit markets) without exposing resting orders to the public.
- **Internalizers** (e.g., wholesalers) execute client orders against their own inventory or against other client flow, sometimes without routing to exchanges.

Executions from dark venues may still appear in trade feeds, but the underlying pre-trade quote information is not available. This creates an interpretability challenge: observed trades may reflect hidden liquidity that never appeared in the visible order book.

An autonomous analyst needs to be aware that:

- Apparent gaps or jumps in lit prices can be smoothed by off-exchange trading.
- Volume reported on the tape may exceed what can be explained by visible depth alone.

Smart Order Routing

Large participants rarely send orders to a single venue. Instead, *smart order routers* (SORs) split and direct orders across venues to:

- Access the best prices across fragmented books.
- Minimize market impact and signaling risk.
- Comply with best-execution and routing rules.

From the perspective of tick data, this means that activity in one venue is coupled to conditions on others. A local pattern in one exchange's feed may only make sense when viewed in the context of the global market.

Frictions and Their Imprint on Data

Textbook finance often assumes frictionless markets and continuous prices. At the microstructural level, several frictions strongly shape the data that an LLM-driven system will see.

Discrete Prices and Ticks

Prices move in discrete increments called *ticks* (the minimum price step allowed by the venue). As a result:

- Small changes in supply or demand may not immediately change the last price; they first change depth at the current best prices.
- Many return values at high frequencies are exactly zero, not because nothing happened, but because trades occurred at the same price.

Any model that treats prices as continuous must keep this discreteness in mind when sampling and aggregating.

Transaction Costs and Slippage

Beyond the spread, traders incur:

- **Explicit costs:** commissions, fees, taxes.
- **Implicit costs:** slippage (difference between expected and realized price), market impact (price movement caused by one's own order), and opportunity cost (not getting filled).

These frictions mean that not every predicted price move is economically tradable. An autonomous analyst must evaluate strategies on *net* performance after trading costs; otherwise, high-frequency "profits" may vanish when realistic costs are applied.

Latency and Asynchrony

Market data is not instantaneous:

- Orders take time to reach the exchange and be acknowledged.
- Data feeds reach different recipients at different speeds.
- Different instruments (e.g., stock vs. related future) may have slightly misaligned timestamps.

This latency creates subtle issues:

- Naïve lead–lag relationships in data may reflect timestamp alignment rather than true predictability.
- Backtests that assume perfect synchronization can overstate achievable performance.

For LLM-based agents that consume both text and tick data, alignment is even more delicate: a news article's *published* timestamp may lag behind the first informed trades reacting to the underlying event.

From Tick Data to Features an LLM Can Understand

Most autonomous analysts will not work directly with every quote and order message. Instead, they will build feature representations that summarize microstructural information.

Common transformations include:

- **Bars:** Aggregating trades into fixed time bars (e.g., 1-minute OHLCV) or volume bars, which smooth idiosyncratic microstructure noise.

- **Microstructure-derived features:**
  - Spread, midprice, and midprice changes.
  - Order book imbalance (relative depth on bid vs. ask).
  - Volumes at and across levels, cancellation rates.
- **Event flags:** Indicators for scheduled events (open, close, auctions, macro announcements) and detected anomalies (spikes in spread or volume).

When these features are fed into an LLM, either directly (as text-encoded features) or via a separate numeric model linked to a text model, they carry imprints of the underlying participants, venues, and frictions discussed above.

The purpose of this section has been to ground those features in market reality. Once you see that every row of data represents a negotiation between buyers and sellers, subject to explicit rules and implicit constraints, it becomes clear why autonomous systems must respect microstructure: not every pattern in the data corresponds to an exploitable signal, and not every predicted move can be traded profitably once spreads, depth, and latency are taken into account.

1.2 Corporate Disclosures, News, and Alternative Data

In the previous section we treated prices and volumes as the visible outcome of a strategic game among different market participants. An autonomous analyst built on large language models (LLMs) will rarely rely on market data alone. To form views on fundamentals, risk, and narrative, it must also digest the *textual* and *semi-structured* information that flows around those trades.

This section describes that informational backbone. We move from the most formal and regulated sources (corporate disclosures) to more fluid and noisy streams (news, social media) and, finally, to alternative data (web traffic, transactions, geolocation, satellite imagery, and others). Throughout, we emphasize two questions that matter for LLM-based systems:

- How is the information *produced and structured* in the real world?
- What legal, ethical, and technical constraints shape how an autonomous system may *ingest, store, and use* it?

By the end of this section, you should have a mental map of where key text and semi-structured signals come from, what they *really* look like in raw form, and what "compliant ingestion" means in practice.

The Regulated Backbone: Corporate Disclosures

Public companies and many issuers are required by law to disclose material information in standardized formats. These disclosures form the foundation of most fundamental analysis and are also the safest starting point for an autonomous analyst, because:

- They are public and broadly accessible.
- Their content, timing, and structure follow relatively clear rules.
- They come with explicit identifiers (company IDs, filing types, dates) that anchor other data.

Although regulatory frameworks differ across jurisdictions, the core ideas are similar. We will use the terminology of a typical major jurisdiction as a concrete example, but the concepts generalize.

Periodic Reports: Annuals and Quarterlies

Most listed companies must publish:

- An **annual report** with audited financial statements and extensive narrative discussion.
- One or more **interim reports** (quarterly or semiannual), usually reviewed rather than fully audited, with updated financials and commentary.

From an LLM's perspective, these documents are rich, multi-layered inputs:

Structured sections. Regardless of local naming, periodic reports typically contain:

- *Financial statements*: income statement, balance sheet, cash flow statement, statement of changes in equity, each with comparative periods.
- *Notes*: detailed explanations, accounting policies, segment breakdowns, and risk disclosures.
- *Management discussion and analysis (MD&A)* or similar: narrative explaining performance, strategy, and outlook.
- *Risk factors* and *forward-looking statements*: standardized language about uncertainties and legal caveats.

These sections are not only readable by humans; they are also amenable to machine parsing. Headings and item numbers often follow templates, which makes it easier to build extractors that separate tables from prose and tag specific topics (liquidity, capital expenditures, regulatory risk, etc.) before submitting them to an LLM.

Timing conventions. Periodic reports are tied to fixed calendars:

- They refer to a specific reporting period (e.g., year ending December 31).
- They are filed within defined deadlines after that period ends.

This creates a natural lag between the *economic reality* and its *official description*. An autonomous analyst must respect this lag. When building features or backtests, you should only let the system "see" a filing from its actual publication timestamp onward; using its content to explain or predict events that occurred before publication is a form of look-ahead bias.

Current Reports and Event-Driven Filings

Not all material information fits neatly into periodic cycles. Companies are often required to disclose significant events as they occur, via *current reports*. Examples include:

- Major acquisitions or divestitures.
- Changes in senior management or auditors.
- Defaults, restructurings, or material impairments.
- Significant legal actions or regulatory investigations.

These documents are typically shorter and more focused than full reports, but they are important for autonomous analysis:

- They mark specific event timestamps (announcement of a merger, regulatory fine, etc.).
- They provide structured labels that can help an LLM classify other unstructured content (e.g., news stories about the same event).

In raw form, event-driven filings may be text-heavy or include embedded PDFs and scanned attachments. Practical ingestion pipelines must normalize formats (e.g., convert PDFs to text, handle images of tables) and recover clean timestamps and identifiers.

Prospectuses and Offering Documents

When companies issue new securities (equity, debt, structured products), they publish prospectuses or offering memoranda. These documents explain:

- The terms of the securities (coupon, maturity, covenants, voting rights).
- Use of proceeds.

- Detailed risk factors and business descriptions.

Prospectuses give LLMs a high-quality, formal definition of the instrument universe. For example, by reading bond covenants or convertible bond terms, an LLM can infer which triggers or scenarios may materially alter payoffs. For an autonomous analyst, these documents are especially useful when mapping new or complex instruments into a standardized conceptual schema.

Identifiers, Schemas, and Machine-Readable Layers

Modern regulators increasingly require or encourage machine-readable submissions:

- Financial statements may be tagged using structured taxonomies (e.g., XBRL-like frameworks).
- Filings carry unique company and security identifiers and standardized fields for dates, periods, and filing types.

For LLM-based systems, you rarely want to process disclosures as raw monolithic text. Instead:

- Use the structured layer (tags, identifiers) to anchor each text snippet to a company, instrument, period, and concept.
- Feed the textual content with this structured metadata as part of the prompt or as side-channel features.

This combination allows an LLM not only to summarize or classify text, but to reason about its meaning in a precise context (e.g., "segment revenue in EMEA fell 10% year-on-year in Q2 2024").

Earnings Communications: Numbers Plus Narrative

Around periodic reports, companies orchestrate a broader earnings communication cycle. This cycle is crucial for understanding short-term price reactions and for training models that connect language to market moves.

Earnings Press Releases

On earnings day, companies typically issue a press release summarizing:

- Key financial metrics (revenue, EPS, margins).
- Non-GAAP adjustments.
- Segment highlights and brief commentary.
- Updated guidance, if provided.

These releases are usually shorter and more digestible than full filings, and they arrive earlier in the day. For autonomous analysis:

- They provide the first structured, machine-parsable view of results.
- They are often disseminated simultaneously across regulatory feeds, company websites, and newswires, enabling cross-checks on timing.

Guidance and Outlook Language

Beyond reported numbers, companies often provide *forward-looking guidance*: revenue ranges, margin targets, or qualitative outlook. The wording of this guidance can be as important as the numbers themselves.

LLMs are naturally well-suited to analyze such text, but you must be careful to:

- Separate *levels* (e.g., "revenue expected to grow mid-single digits") from *changes* (e.g., "previously high-single digits").

- Align guidance language with the time period it refers to (next quarter, full year, multi-year plan).

This requires pre-processing that extracts effective dates and target periods, and often joins multiple documents (prior guidance vs. revised guidance) before asking an LLM to explain the change.

Earnings Calls: Prepared Remarks and Q&A

Earnings calls add a spoken layer, generally split into:

- **Prepared remarks**: scripted commentary by management.
- **Q&A**: unscripted interaction with analysts and, sometimes, investors.

Transcripts (or audio transformed into text) are a gold mine for LLMs:

- They reveal management's tone, confidence, and choice of language.
- Q&A exposes areas where investors are confused, skeptical, or focused on specific risks.

However, transcripts also introduce challenges:

- Speaker attribution must be preserved (CEO vs. CFO vs. analyst).
- Time alignment with market data is fuzzy; early parts of the call may move the price while later questions arrive after the main reaction.
- Automated transcripts may contain errors or mis-tagged speakers.

A robust ingestion pipeline will therefore:

- Normalize transcripts into a structured format: segments with speaker labels, timestamps (where available), and section tags (prepared vs. Q&A).

- Optionally, enrich text with simple acoustic or behavioral cues (e.g., unusually long pauses, corrections), when permissible and available.

News and Research: Professional and Retail Flows

Beyond formal corporate communications, capital markets are saturated with news and commentary. LLM-based systems excel at reading such material, but the volume and noise level are high.

Newswires and Professional Outlets

Traditional newswire services and financial news outlets produce short, time-stamped articles with clear editorial standards. Typical content includes:

- Breaking corporate news (earnings, M&A, management changes).
- Macro news (economic releases, policy decisions, geopolitical events).
- Market color ("stocks rise as ...") and analysis.

For autonomous analysis, the key properties are:

- **Timeliness:** News often arrives close to, or slightly after, the underlying event.
- **Redundancy:** Multiple outlets may cover the same story with different angles and delays.
- **Metadata:** Tickers, regions, topics, and priority flags may be tagged explicitly.

An ingestion system should de-duplicate related articles, align them to common events, and avoid double-counting the same story when building features.

Broker Research and Analyst Reports

Sell-side analysts publish in-depth reports on companies, sectors, and themes. These documents:

- Contain detailed valuation models, forecasts, and scenario analysis.
- Include ratings (buy/hold/sell) and target prices.

Access is often restricted; licensing terms can be strict. For an autonomous analyst, using research in training or live inference requires particular care:

- Ensure you have rights to store and process the content, including for machine learning.
- Keep detailed audit trails of which model was trained on which research packages and under what contractual terms.

Technically, research reports are long-form text with tables and charts. LLMs can help summarize them or extract structured signals (e.g., target price changes, narrative shifts), but heavy pre-processing is usually needed to handle layout, images, and embedded models.

Social Media and Retail Commentary

At the other end of the spectrum lies user-generated content on social platforms, message boards, and chat communities. These streams are:

- Extremely high volume and noisy.
- Full of slang, sarcasm, and non-standard spelling.
- Vulnerable to coordinated campaigns, spam, and manipulation.

Yet they can still matter. Retail-driven episodes have shown that online communities can–at times–coordinate around particular stocks or narratives. LLMs are particularly good at understanding informal language, but:

- You must apply strong filters and spam detection before feeding content into models.
- Ethical and legal constraints around user privacy and terms of service must be respected.

In practice, social data is often best used as a coarse sentiment indicator or as an early-warning signal, rather than as a primary driver of decisions.

Alternative Data: Beyond Traditional Text

Alternative data refers to any non-traditional dataset that provides insight into economic activity, consumer behavior, or corporate performance. It is a broad and evolving category; here we focus on common types and their structure.

Web and App Usage Data

This category includes:

- Website traffic metrics (visits, unique users, time on site).
- App usage metrics (daily active users, session counts, retention).

Such data is often collected from panels, browser extensions, app SDKs, or proxies. It is typically:

- Provided at a regular frequency (daily, weekly, monthly).
- Aggregated at some level (domain, app, region).

From an LLM's perspective, web/app data is mostly numeric rather than textual. However, it can be integrated with text by:

- Annotating disclosures and news with concurrent usage trends.
- Asking an LLM to interpret divergences (e.g., "management claims strong engagement, but alternative data shows declining daily active users").

Geolocation and Footfall Data

Location data from mobile devices or other sensors can estimate:

- Store visits and foot traffic for retailers.
- Construction activity, port congestion, or factory utilization.

Typical characteristics:

- **Granularity:** Observations at the device or visit level, later aggregated to store, city, or region.
- **Sampling bias:** Only users who opt in or use specific apps are observed; coverage can vary by region and demographic.

These biases must be modeled carefully. Autonomous analysts should avoid treating alternative data as ground truth. Instead, it is another noisy, partial view of reality, to be triangulated with official disclosures and other sources.

Transaction and Receipt Data

Aggregated credit card, debit card, or receipt-scanning data can provide near-real-time estimates of sales for consumer companies. These datasets typically include:

- Merchant identifiers or categories.
- Transaction counts and amounts over time.

Again, coverage is partial (limited banks, regions, or consumer segments), and legal constraints are strict:

- Data must be anonymized and aggregated to protect individual privacy.
- Use must comply with local data-protection regulations.

LLMs may not process raw transaction rows directly, but they can interpret aggregations (e.g., "inferred same-store sales grew 8% year-on-year in October") in the context of company commentary.

Satellite, Image, and Sensor Data

Imagery of parking lots, shipping lanes, crop fields, or infrastructure can be transformed into quantitative indicators through computer vision and other models. For an LLM-centric pipeline:

- The heavy lifting is usually done by specialized models that convert raw images into counts or indices.
- LLMs then reason over those derived metrics alongside text.

For example, an LLM could be prompted with: "Satellite-based store-traffic index for Company X has declined three months in a row, while management emphasizes 'strong momentum'. Analyze the discrepancy."

Compliance, Governance, and MNPI

Powerful as these data sources are, they operate within strict legal and ethical boundaries. A central concern is **material nonpublic information** (MNPI): information that is both material (a reasonable investor would consider it important) and not publicly available.

Avoiding MNPI in Autonomous Systems

LLM-based analysts must be designed so that:

- Training and inference data do not contain MNPI.
- The system cannot be tricked into inferring or leaking MNPI from other internal systems.

Practical safeguards include:

- Restricting inputs to approved, licensed, and demonstrably public datasets.

- Segregating environments: for example, using separate models or instances for proprietary data, with access controls and logging.
- Implementing red-teaming and testing to ensure that the model does not memorize or regurgitate sensitive documents used during fine-tuning.

Licensing, Retention, and Auditability

Even publicly available or alternative data may come with contractual limitations:

- Some licenses allow human use but restrict machine learning or derivative works.
- Retention policies may limit how long data can be stored or used in models.

An autonomous analyst must therefore be embedded in a broader *governance framework* that:

- Tracks the provenance of each dataset and its licensing terms.
- Logs which models were trained on which sources and when.
- Provides audit trails for regulators, clients, and internal risk functions.

From a system-design perspective, this suggests a layered architecture: a centralized data catalog and access layer; a feature store that exposes only compliant, derived signals; and LLMs that operate on those signals rather than scraping arbitrary content themselves.

Designing Ingestion Pipelines for LLMs

Bringing these pieces together, what does a good ingestion pipeline look like for an autonomous LLM-based analyst?

Normalize and Anchor

First, normalize each source to a consistent schema:

- Map companies to unique identifiers.
- Standardize timestamps to a common time zone and format.
- Tag documents with type (annual report, earnings call transcript, news article, research note, social post) and key attributes (language, length, jurisdiction).

This anchoring allows you to join text with market data and alternative signals around specific events and periods.

Segment and Structure Text

Second, break large documents into meaningful segments:

- By section in filings (MD&A, risk factors, notes).
- By speaker and topic in transcripts.
- By story and event in news flows.

Each segment becomes a text unit with attached metadata. LLMs can then be prompted with focused questions about each unit or retrieve relevant segments via embeddings when answering broader queries.

Enrich with Numeric and Categorical Features

Third, augment text with key numeric and categorical context:

- Actual figures (revenue, EPS), deltas vs. prior periods, and consensus expectations.
- Alternative data indicators (web traffic growth, transaction trends).

- Microstructure features around the event window (abnormal volume, volatility).

These can be fed as structured inputs alongside the text, allowing the LLM to reason about language *and* numbers jointly.

Enforce Governance and Monitoring

Finally, wrap the ingestion and modeling process in governance:

- Validate sources for licensing, privacy, and MNPI constraints before ingestion.
- Version data and models, and log queries and outputs for later review.
- Continuously monitor for drift in data distributions and narratives (for example, when disclosure practices change or new alt-data sources are introduced).

In this way, the autonomous analyst becomes not just a powerful consumer of text and data, but a well-governed component within a broader institutional framework.

The next section will turn from the cross-sectional richness of these data sources to their temporal behavior. We will examine how the properties of financial time series—nonstationarity, volatility clustering, and regime shifts—interact with the flows of disclosures, news, and alternative data we have just described, and what that implies for training and evaluating autonomous models over time.

1.3 Time Series Characteristics and Market Regimes

Up to this point we have focused on *what* is traded, *who* trades, and *what they say* in disclosures and news. We now turn to *how prices and volumes evolve over time*. For an autonomous analyst, this is where statistical reality collides with model assumptions.

Many introductory treatments assume that prices or returns behave like a simple random walk with independent, normally distributed increments. Real markets are more complicated. Empirical financial time series exhibit several robust patterns:

- Price levels are **nonstationary**: their average level wanders over time.
- Returns have **heavy tails**: large moves happen more often than in a normal distribution.
- Volatility **clusters**: quiet periods alternate with storms.
- Markets switch between **regimes**: qualitatively different environments with distinct behavior.

This section explains these properties in intuitive terms, shows how they appear in data, and discusses why regime awareness is essential when training and evaluating LLM-driven trading systems.

From Prices to Returns and Volatility

LLM-based analysts will usually see price and volume series pre-processed into features such as returns and realized volatility. Understanding these basic transformations is the first step.

Price Levels vs. Returns

A price series P_t (for example, daily closing prices) is often transformed into returns:

- **Simple return** between time $t-1$ and t: roughly the percentage gain or loss.
- **Log return**: the difference in log prices, which adds more nicely over time.

Conceptually, you can think of a price series as "where we are" and a return series as "how much we moved" in each period.

This distinction matters because:

- Price levels tend to drift upward or downward over long horizons, driven by growth, inflation, and discount rates.
- Returns, particularly short-horizon log returns, are closer to a stationary series whose distribution and typical scale are more stable over time.

Most statistical modeling — including the inputs to many learning systems — works with returns rather than raw prices for this reason.

Realized Volatility as a Time Series

Volatility is the magnitude of price fluctuations. It is not directly observed but can be estimated from data. At a basic level, we can think of a daily volatility proxy as:

- The standard deviation of intraday returns, or
- A function of intraday high, low, open, and close, or
- The absolute value or square of daily returns, used as a simple volatility indicator.

Whatever the precise formula, volatility itself forms a time series. Understanding how this series behaves — whether it is stable, clustered, or regime-dependent — is critical for risk management and for assessing how a model will perform under stress.

Nonstationarity: Markets That Do Not Sit Still

A time series is called *stationary* if its statistical properties (like mean and variance) are stable over time. Financial price levels are typically *not* stationary.

Wandering Levels and Changing Trends

Consider a broad equity index over many years. Its level moves as economies grow, inflation accumulates, and risk appetite changes. There is no fixed long-run "average price" it oscillates around. Instead:

- Long bull markets produce persistent uptrends.
- Bear markets or crises produce sharp declines and sometimes prolonged flat periods.

This **nonstationary** behavior poses a problem for models that assume constant distributions. For example:

- A model trained during a long bull run may implicitly assume that upward drifts are typical and underweight the probability of a prolonged drawdown.
- A volatility estimate based on a calm period may drastically understate risk in a crisis regime.

For autonomous analysts, the implication is clear: you must check whether the world your model was trained in resembles the world it is being asked to act in now.

Returns: Closer to Stationary, But Not Perfect

Returns are *more* stationary than prices, but still not ideal:

- Mean returns can vary over time (e.g., risk premia change).
- The variance of returns (volatility) changes — sometimes dramatically.

This means that even if you model returns rather than prices, you should be wary of assuming fixed statistical parameters. Many classical models (and most backtests) implicitly assume some form of stationarity; real markets only approximately satisfy that assumption, and only over limited windows.

Heavy Tails: Extreme Moves Happen More Often

If daily returns were normally distributed, extreme moves (say, more than 5 standard deviations) would be vanishingly rare. In practice, they happen orders of magnitude more often than the normal model predicts. This is what we mean by **heavy tails**.

Intuitive Picture of Heavy Tails

Plotting a histogram of returns, you often see:

- A central peak that is somewhat bell-shaped.
- "Fat" shoulders and tails: more observations far from zero than a normal curve with the same variance would have.

Intuitively, markets have more outliers and jumps than a simple random-walk model. Crashes, panics, and sudden repricings of information are part of normal market life, not once-in-a-millennium events.

For autonomous analysts, heavy tails have several implications:

- Risk estimates based on normal assumptions will understate tail risk.
- Models trained mostly on typical days may perform very poorly on extreme days, precisely when decisions matter most.
- Evaluation metrics that average performance across all days may hide catastrophic failures in the tails.

LLM-based systems that reason about scenarios must therefore be prompted and tested explicitly on rare but plausible events, not just on average days.

Volatility Clustering: Calm and Storms

One of the most robust empirical facts about financial time series is **volatility clustering**: large moves tend to be followed by large moves (not necessarily in the same direction), and small moves by small moves.

What Volatility Clustering Looks Like

If you plot a series of daily returns, it may look irregular. Now imagine plotting the *absolute* returns or squared returns. You will often see:

- Stretches where absolute returns are consistently low — quiet markets.
- Stretches where absolute returns are consistently high — turbulent markets.

This pattern shows that volatility behaves like a slow-moving state variable. It drifts up and down in clusters, instead of being independently resampled every day.

Short Memory in Returns, Long Memory in Volatility

An important nuance is that:

- Raw returns themselves often show very little autocorrelation beyond the very short term; predicting tomorrow's *direction* from past directions is hard.
- Measures of volatility, however, can show persistent autocorrelation; knowing that volatility is high today tells you it is likely to remain elevated for some time.

This has practical consequences:

- Volatility-sensitive strategies (e.g., options, risk-parity allocations) should condition on volatility states.
- Backtests should consider whether a strategy implicitly assumes a particular volatility environment. A strategy tuned on calm markets may break in turbulent regimes.

Market Regimes: Distinct States of the World

Nonstationarity, heavy tails, and volatility clustering all point to a deeper idea: markets operate in different **regimes**. A regime is a period during which market behavior is qualitatively different — like weather patterns rather than random noise.

Examples of Regimes

Common regime distinctions include:

- **Calm vs. stressed:** low volatility, tight spreads, modest volumes versus high volatility, wide spreads, and heavy trading.
- **Risk-on vs. risk-off:** environments where investors collectively seek riskier assets versus ones where they flee to safety.
- **Liquidity-rich vs. liquidity-poor:** periods with abundant depth and easy financing versus those with constrained funding and thin order books.

Regimes are not always obvious, and different assets can be in different regimes at the same time. Nonetheless, the concept is useful because many relationships (correlations, betas, reaction to news) change materially between regimes.

Simple Ways to Identify Regimes

There are many formal models for regime detection, but before we go there, it is useful to think in simple, transparent terms. For example:

- Threshold-based rules: label days as "high volatility" if volatility exceeds some percentile, or as "stress" if spreads and funding rates are elevated.
- Event-based regimes: mark windows around crises, policy changes, or major macro shocks as distinct environments.

- Clustering: group days into clusters based on features like volatility, cross-asset correlations, and volume.

For building and evaluating autonomous analysts, you do not always need a perfect, fully automated regime classifier. Even coarse labels can be very helpful when:

- Segmenting historical data into training, validation, and test regimes.

- Stress-testing models on specific periods.

- Conditioning LLM prompts on the current state (for example, "we are in a high-volatility environment; assess the robustness of this strategy").

A Visual Tour of Key Properties

To make these ideas concrete, consider the following schematic example: a single synthetic price series over time, its corresponding returns, and a volatility proxy.

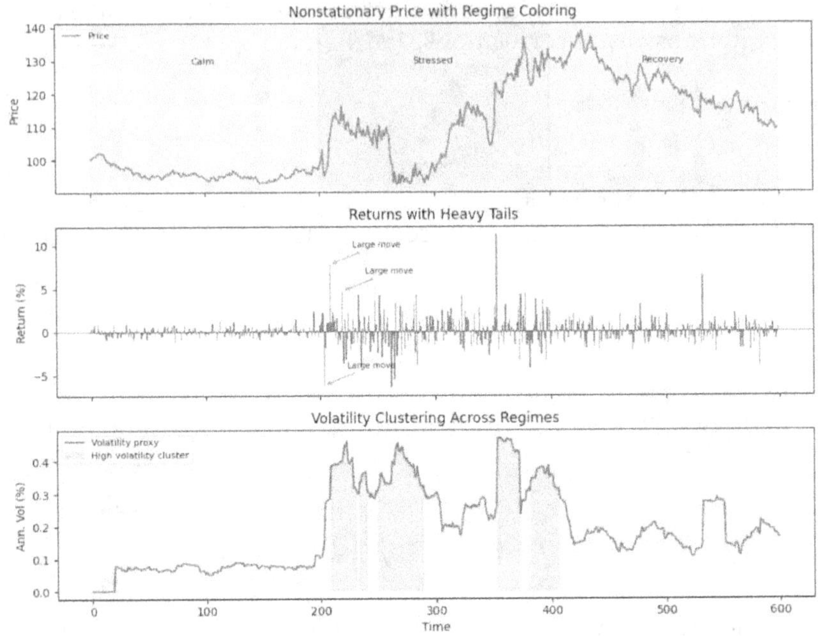

The top panel illustrates:

- A **nonstationary** price path that drifts differently across three regimes.
- Regime coloring, which reminds us that the same statistical tools may behave differently in each segment.

The middle panel shows:

- Returns with many small moves and a few outsized spikes, highlighting **heavy tails**.

The bottom panel emphasizes:

- A volatility proxy that is low in calm periods, high in stressed periods, and intermediate in recovery.

- Clear **volatility clustering** and its alignment with regimes.

In your own work, you should produce similar visual checks for any asset or strategy you care about. They are a quick way to see whether your modeling assumptions stand a chance of being realistic.

Sampling, Seasonality, and Calendar Effects

So far we have talked mainly about daily data. At intraday or higher frequencies, another layer of structure appears: **seasonality**.

Intraday Patterns

Within a typical trading day, many markets exhibit a U-shaped volatility and volume pattern:

- High activity and volatility near the open, as participants digest overnight news and adjust positions.
- A quieter mid-day lull.
- Rising activity near the close, as traders rebalance and benchmark-constrained investors execute.

For high-frequency autonomous agents, ignoring this intraday pattern can be as damaging as ignoring long-term regimes. A model trained on mid-day behavior may fail badly if applied to the open or close.

Calendar Effects and Event Time

There are also weekly, monthly, and event-driven regularities:

- Differences in behavior across days of the week or month-ends.
- Predictable spikes around macroeconomic announcements, central bank meetings, or major earnings days.

From an LLM system's perspective, calendar and event metadata are important conditioning variables. When you ask an autonomous analyst to interpret a price move, you should tell it whether the move occurred during a major macro release, at the open, or in the mid-day lull; the same numerical move may have very different significance depending on context.

Implications for Modeling and Evaluation

Understanding these time-series properties is not an academic exercise. They directly affect how you train, validate, and monitor autonomous analysts.

Rolling vs. Expanding Windows

Because data-generating processes drift, many practitioners use:

- **Rolling windows**: train on a sliding window of recent data, so the model reflects current conditions.
- **Expanding windows**: train on all data up to a point, giving more weight to long history.

For autonomous systems, you will typically combine these with:

- Explicit regime conditioning (e.g., including volatility state as a feature).
- Periodic re-training or fine-tuning schedules that respect data availability and operational constraints.

The key is to avoid naïvely training on decades of data and assuming that the resulting model is equally valid in all future regimes.

Walk-Forward Validation and Leakage Risks

Backtesting must mimic the information flow experienced in real time:

- Use **walk-forward** validation: at each step, train on past data only, then test on a forward period.
- Prevent **information leakage**: do not use future information (including future regimes, future volatility estimates, or revised data) when constructing features for past periods.

For LLM-based analysts that consume both text and numerical data, leakage can be subtle. Examples include:

- Using a final, restated annual report to explain or predict market reactions that occurred before the restatement.
- Feeding the model a news summary that includes hindsight commentary about events that were not known at the time.

A regime-aware backtest ensures that the model is evaluated on realistic sequences of calm and stressed periods, with only contemporaneous information available at each point.

Regime-Aware Performance Evaluation

Instead of reporting a single aggregate performance number, you should measure strategy and model behavior by regime:

- Returns, risk, and error metrics in calm versus stressed periods.
- Sensitivity to volatility, liquidity conditions, and cross-asset correlations.

For an autonomous analyst, you might ask:

- Does the model's accuracy in interpreting earnings news degrade in high-volatility regimes?
- Does the agent over-trade or under-react when spreads widen?
- Are certain prompts or decision policies only safe in specific environments?

By breaking evaluation down this way, you gain insight into where the model can be trusted and where human oversight or additional safeguards are essential.

Tracking Distribution Shift in LLM-Based Systems

Finally, LLMs themselves are statistical models trained on large corpora. Their behavior can become misaligned with current markets when the underlying distributions shift.

Shifts in Language and Disclosure

Over time:

- Corporate reporting standards evolve.
- New business models and terms (for example, in digital assets or climate-related disclosures) emerge.
- Regulatory changes alter what firms must disclose and how they phrase risks.

An LLM fine-tuned on older disclosures might misinterpret newer phrasing or fail to recognize subtle shifts in tone that are meaningful under current norms.

Shifts in Market Structure and Behavior

Similarly, the statistical properties of returns, volumes, and cross-asset relationships can change due to:

- Structural changes in liquidity provision, regulation, or technology.
- Long-lasting macro shocks that reshape risk premia.

An autonomous analyst that internally assumes "typical" volatility or tail behavior from one era may be dangerously wrong in another. Ongoing monitoring of input distributions and model outputs is therefore necessary, along with periodic re-training and explicit stress-testing under alternative regimes.

In summary, real-world financial time series are nonstationary, heavy-tailed, and volatility-clustered, with behavior that shifts across distinct regimes. For LLM-powered autonomous analysts, regime awareness is not optional; it is a prerequisite for honest backtesting, robust deployment, and meaningful risk control. In the following chapters, we will build on these foundations to design model architectures, prompting strategies, and evaluation frameworks that respect the empirical realities of markets instead of fighting them.

Chapter 2

Quantitative and ML Foundations

Before we can trust an autonomous analyst, we must understand the language it speaks: vectors and gradients, probabilities and losses, signals and noise. This chapter forges that shared language-linking core math, statistics, and machine learning ideas directly to the everyday realities of slippage, regime shifts, and overfit backtests-so that every later model feels less like a black box and more like a negotiable trading partner.

2.1 Probability, Statistics, and Uncertainty Quantification

Machine-learning models, factor screens, and even simple backtests all operate on the same raw material: noisy financial data. Prices jump on news, spreads widen or tighten without warning, and what worked last year may quietly decay. To use large models and transformers intelligently in this environment, you need more than coding skills—you need a probabilistic mindset.

This section develops that mindset. We will not try to turn you into a mathematician; instead, we will build a practical vocabulary for thinking about randomness, uncertainty, and sampling error in markets. The goal is that when your model reports a Sharpe ratio of 1.3, or a win rate of 56%, you can immediately ask: "How uncertain is that number? Could it be luck? How much capital should I trust to it?"

Random Variables: Returns as Draws from a Distribution

Prices and returns are not fixed quantities; they are outcomes of a process that could have unfolded differently. The same model run on different historical windows, or on a slightly different universe of assets, will produce slightly different performance. The language we use for this is *random variables* and *distributions*.

Think of daily log-returns of a stock, or the daily PnL of your strategy, as coming from a "return generator." Each day, the generator outputs a number: sometimes positive, sometimes negative, usually small, occasionally very large in magnitude. If we could rewind time and replay the world many times, we would see a spread of possible sequences and a spread of possible PnL paths. The distribution describes how often different outcomes occur across these hypothetical replays.

Key ideas:

- **Random variable:** A number whose value is not known in advance, because it depends on uncertain events (for example, tomorrow's PnL).
- **Distribution:** A description of how likely different values of the random variable are (for example, small losses are common, huge gains are rare).
- **Outcome vs. process:** What you observe is one particular outcome from the process; the distribution is about the process itself.

For most of this book, the main random variables you care about will be:

- Asset returns (single-period or multi-period).
- Strategy PnL at a given horizon (daily, weekly, etc.).
- Performance metrics calculated from those, such as Sharpe ratio.

Adopting the probabilistic mindset means that you stop treating a backtest as "the truth" and start treating it as one sample from many possible histories.

Expectations, Variance, and Correlation in Trading Language

Once we accept that returns are random variables, we need a compact way to talk about their "typical" size, variability, and co-movement.

Expectation (average outcome).

The *expected value* of a random variable is the long-run average outcome if the underlying process were repeated many times. In trading language:

- Expected return is the average return per period, across many hypothetical repetitions of history.
- Your *sample mean* return (the average of the returns you observed in your data) is an estimate of that expected return.

If you say your strategy has an "edge" of 10 basis points per day, you are implicitly claiming that the expected return of the PnL distribution is +0.10%.

Variance and volatility (spread of outcomes).

Variance measures how widely the outcomes spread around their average. The square root of variance is volatility. In practice:

- Higher volatility means a more "jagged" equity curve, greater swings in daily PnL, and larger drawdowns for the same average return.

- The sample standard deviation of your returns is an estimate of the true volatility of the process.

Volatility is not inherently bad; a high-Sharpe strategy might also have high volatility if its expected return is even higher. What matters is the trade-off.

Covariance and correlation (moving together).

If you run many signals or strategies, you care not only about each one's behavior in isolation but also about how they behave jointly:

- *Covariance* measures whether two random variables tend to be above or below their means at the same time.
- *Correlation* is a rescaled version of covariance that lies between -1 and +1 and is easier to interpret:

- +1 means they move perfectly together (no diversification benefit).
- 0 means their movements are unrelated (some diversification).
- -1 means they move perfectly in opposite directions (strong hedge).

A probabilistic view of correlation keeps you honest about diversification. Two signals that "look different" in their formula may be strongly positively correlated in their realized PnL, providing much less diversification than you hoped.

Gaussian vs. Heavy-Tailed Worlds

A common simplifying assumption in finance and machine learning is that returns follow a normal (Gaussian) distribution. Gaussian distributions are convenient:

- They are fully described by just a mean and a variance.
- Many estimators and confidence intervals are particularly simple under Gaussian assumptions.

However, real financial returns often show:

- **Heavy tails:** Extreme moves (large gains or losses) occur more often than a Gaussian distribution would predict.
- **Skewness:** The distribution may be lopsided, with more frequent large losses than large gains (or vice versa).

For example, a Gaussian model might say that a 5-sigma daily move should be virtually impossible in your lifetime, yet we observe such moves in markets. For an autonomous analyst, the lesson is:

> Do not trust models that rely on thin tails when you are managing tail risk.

You can still use Gaussian-based methods as rough approximations, but you must be aware that they can underestimate the likelihood and impact of large drawdowns.

Sampling: From Theoretical Process to Observed Data

Your theoretical return generator is unobservable. What you actually have is a finite sample of data: maybe 2,000 daily returns (about eight years), or 500 weekly returns (about ten years). Statistical thinking is about how to use such finite samples to learn about the underlying process, and how to understand the error in that learning.

i.i.d. assumptions vs. serial dependence.

Many textbook results assume that your returns are:

- *Independent:* Yesterday's return tells you nothing about today's.
- *Identically distributed:* The distribution of returns is the same every day (same mean, same variance).

These are referred to as i.i.d. (independent and identically distributed) observations. In markets, this is rarely strictly true:

- There is often **serial dependence**: volatility clusters; trending or mean-reverting behavior can occur.
- There are **regime changes**: the distribution of returns in a crisis is very different from that in a calm bull market.

Nevertheless, i.i.d. assumptions are often used as a first approximation, especially for daily or weekly returns of a reasonably diversified strategy. As you build more sophisticated models (such as GARCH or sequence models), you will explicitly model dependence and regime changes. For uncertainty quantification, you must always keep in mind whether the tools you are using rely on i.i.d. assumptions.

Stationarity vs. regime changes.

A process is called *stationary* if its statistical properties (such as mean and variance) are stable over time. In practice:

- If your strategy changed execution logic, or the microstructure of the market changed (new tick sizes, new regulations), your past PnL distribution may no longer be a good guide to the future.
- If a central bank moved from a low-rate to a high-rate regime, factor behavior may also change.

When you compute statistics from historical data, you are implicitly assuming that the future is "similar enough" to the past window you used. This is a judgment call that statistics cannot solve for you, but the probabilistic mindset forces you to articulate that assumption.

Law of large numbers and what it really means.

The law of large numbers says that, under suitable conditions, the sample average of i.i.d. random variables converges to the true expectation as the sample size grows. Translated:

- If your strategy has a true Sharpe ratio of 1, and you sample more and more days, your estimated Sharpe will settle closer and closer to 1.
- With only a small number of observations, your estimated Sharpe can easily be very far from the true Sharpe, simply because of chance.

What the law of large numbers does *not* say:

- It does not say that past losses guarantee future gains.
- It does not say that a high Sharpe in a short window must be close to the true Sharpe.

For trading, the core insight is that with limited data, your apparent edge is noisy. You must quantify that noise.

Estimating Edge: Point Estimates and Their Limitations

When you take a finite sample of returns and compute quantities such as average return, volatility, or correlation, you are computing *point estimates*. These are your best guesses of the underlying true parameters, based on the data you have.

Examples of point estimates.

- Sample mean return per day or per month.
- Sample volatility (standard deviation of returns).
- Sample correlation between two strategies.
- Sample Sharpe ratio (mean divided by standard deviation).

These are straightforward to compute, and modern libraries do it for you automatically. The danger is that it is easy to forget they are only estimates. Two different samples from the same process can give noticeably different estimates.

For example, a strategy with a true Sharpe of 1 might easily show a realized Sharpe of 1.8 in one three-year period and 0.2 in another three-year period, just by luck. If you only saw the first period, you would be tempted to massively allocate capital to it, without realizing how much of that performance could be noise.

From Point Estimates to Intervals: Quantifying Uncertainty

To tame this uncertainty, we turn point estimates into *interval estimates*: ranges of plausible values for the true parameter, given the data.

Confidence intervals: what they do and do not say.

A confidence interval for a parameter (for example, mean return) is an interval constructed from your sample, such that if you were to repeat the sampling process many times, a certain percentage (typically 95%) of those intervals would contain the true parameter.

For example:

- You estimate a strategy's annualized Sharpe to be 1.0.
- Based on the amount of data and assumptions about the distribution, you compute a 95% confidence interval of [0.2, 1.8].

Interpretation:

- Given the data you have, Sharpe ratios as low as 0.2 and as high as 1.8 are statistically plausible.
- You should not act as if 1.0 were exact; your capital-at-risk decisions should be robust to this range.

Note what you *cannot* say: you cannot say there is a 95% probability that the true Sharpe lies in that particular interval; that would be a Bayesian statement, which requires specifying a prior belief. The frequentist interpretation is more subtle: 95% of intervals computed this way over many hypothetical samples would cover the true value.

In practice, traders often reason in an intuitive, quasi-Bayesian way: they look at the interval and say, "It is likely in this range." That is fine as long as you understand that the width of the interval reflects the amount of information in your data.

Narrow vs. wide intervals.

The width of a confidence interval is driven by:

- The amount of data (more data generally shrink the interval).
- The variability in the data (more volatile series yield wider intervals).
- The chosen confidence level (99% intervals are wider than 90%).

A wide interval is not a failure; it is an honest statement that, given the volatility and sample size, you cannot pin down the parameter more precisely. This is often the case in high-frequency and short-history strategies.

Sampling Distributions and PnL Uncertainty

Behind every confidence interval is a *sampling distribution*—the distribution of the estimator itself, across hypothetical repeat samples. For example, if you repeatedly sample 1,000 daily returns from the same underlying process and compute the Sharpe ratio each time, the resulting Sharpe estimates will form their own distribution.

Understanding this distribution is crucial when you judge model performance:

- If your model's Sharpe estimate is 1.3 and a simple benchmark's Sharpe is 1.0, you need to know whether 1.3 is meaningfully higher or within expected fluctuation.
- Two backtests that differ by 0.2 or 0.3 in Sharpe may be statistically indistinguishable, depending on data length and volatility.

In later chapters, we will estimate sampling distributions via bootstrapping and Bayesian methods, but the conceptual point is already useful: any performance metric you compute (mean return, Sharpe, drawdown) is itself a random variable with its own distribution.

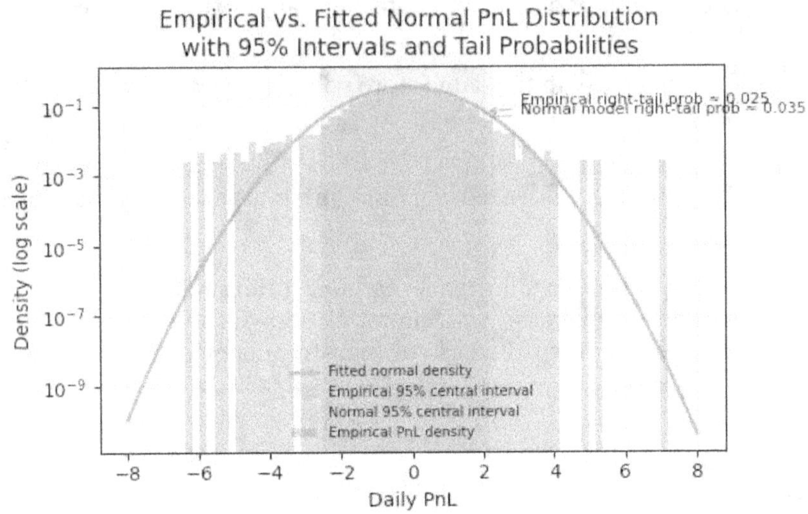

This figure illustrates three key points:

- Your empirical PnL distribution may deviate from a fitted normal curve, especially in the tails.
- Confidence intervals based on the normal approximation can understate the probability of large moves.
- Quantifying tail probabilities explicitly is essential for risk management; do not judge a strategy only by its mean and standard deviation.

Hypothesis Testing: A Discipline Against Fooling Yourself

Once you can describe and quantify uncertainty in estimates, you can pose sharper questions. For example:

- Does this new feature really improve performance, or is the gain just noise?

- Is the Sharpe of model A meaningfully higher than that of model B?
- Is the mean return of a strategy statistically different from zero?

Hypothesis testing is a structured way to answer such questions.

Null and alternative hypotheses.

You start with a simple, skeptical statement–the *null hypothesis*. For example:

- Null: "The true mean return is zero" (no edge).
- Alternative: "The true mean return is greater than zero" (positive edge).

You then ask: if the null were true, how surprising would it be to see the data I actually observed?

Test statistic and p-value.

A *test statistic* is a number computed from your data (for example, a t-statistic for the mean) whose sampling distribution under the null is known or approximated. The *p-value* is:

> The probability, assuming the null hypothesis is true, of obtaining a test statistic at least as extreme as the one observed.

If the p-value is very small (for example, 0.01), it means that seeing such a strong result would be rare if the null were true; this is evidence against the null. In trading practice, you might require very low p-values before trusting that a discovered edge is real, especially when you know you are testing many ideas.

Power and the cost of missing real edges.

Power is the probability that your test correctly rejects a false null hypothesis. In other words, it is your ability to detect a real effect when it exists. Low power means:

- You often fail to recognize genuine alpha signals.

- You may dismiss promising ideas simply because you did not have enough data, or the signal-to-noise ratio was low.

Data length, volatility, and the size of the true effect all affect power. Understanding this forces humility: if you have only a few years of noisy data, even a real effect may not show statistically strong evidence.

Multiple testing, p-hacking, and data snooping.

In a modern ML workflow, you rarely test a single idea. You generate many signals, try many architectures, tune many hyperparameters. If you run hundreds or thousands of experiments, even purely random noise will sometimes look impressive purely by chance.

- *Multiple testing* means that the more hypotheses you test, the more likely you are to find at least one spuriously significant result.
- *P-hacking* is the practice of trying many variations and selectively reporting only the ones with low p-values.
- *Data snooping* occurs when you repeatedly mine the same historical dataset until you find patterns that may not generalize.

A disciplined autonomous analyst acknowledges and mitigates this:

- Use separate holdout periods or markets that are not touched during model development.
- Adjust significance thresholds or use methods that control for multiple testing.
- Place more weight on economic intuition and cross-regime robustness than on a single impressive p-value.

Bootstrapping and Bayesian Perspectives

Classical confidence intervals and tests rely on analytical formulas and assumptions (for example, approximately normal sampling distributions). Two complementary approaches help you go beyond those constraints.

Bootstrapping: re-sampling your data.

Bootstrapping builds an empirical approximation to the sampling distribution of a statistic by repeatedly re-sampling from your observed data:

1. Take your historical returns.
2. Sample with replacement from them to create many pseudo-histories.
3. Compute your performance metric (mean, Sharpe, drawdown) for each pseudo-history.

The resulting distribution of metric values is an estimate of the sampling distribution. This gives you:

- Empirical confidence intervals that may be more robust to non-normality or heteroskedasticity.
- A better sense of the range of outcomes your model might deliver, even under the same underlying process.

Bootstrapping has its own assumptions (for example, that the resampling scheme preserves important dependence structures), but it is often a practical tool when analytical formulas are not trustworthy.

Bayesian vs. frequentist: uncertainty as a belief.

Frequentist methods (confidence intervals, p-values) interpret probability as long-run frequencies under repeated sampling. Bayesian methods treat probability as a degree of belief, allowing you to combine prior information with observed data.

For example:

- Prior: "Most new strategies I try have true Sharpe between -0.5 and 0.5."
- Data: A backtest shows a sample Sharpe of 1.0 over three years.

A Bayesian update would yield a *posterior distribution* over the true Sharpe that balances your prior skepticism with the new evidence. In many realistic settings, this posterior would still place a lot of mass on moderate Sharpe values, reflecting both data noise and prior knowledge that high Sharpe strategies are rare.

Whether or not you implement full Bayesian machinery, thinking this way helps prevent overconfidence. It reminds you that "extraordinary Sharpe ratios require extraordinary evidence."

From Statistical Uncertainty to Risk Limits and Position Sizing

All of this analysis matters only if it shapes decisions. The ultimate goal of uncertainty quantification is to connect backtests and forecasts to concrete risk management rules.

Predictive intervals for PnL.

Instead of saying "expected daily PnL is 0.1% with volatility 1%," you can phrase your expectations as:

> On a typical day, there is a 95% chance that PnL will fall between -X and +Y.

Where X and Y come from your estimated distribution, possibly adjusted for heavy tails. These predictive intervals are directly useful for:

- Setting daily loss limits.
- Stress-testing liquidity and margin needs.
- Communicating realistic expectations to stakeholders.

Position sizing with uncertainty in edge.

Suppose your strategy's annualized Sharpe estimate is 1.0, with a 95% confidence interval of [0.2, 1.8]. If you size positions as if the Sharpe were certainly 1.8, you will likely be over-levered. A more prudent approach is to:

- Size based on a conservative estimate (for example, the lower end or a slightly above-zero quantile of the interval).
- Scale up only as more data accumulate and the uncertainty band tightens.

In other words, you translate statistical uncertainty into operational conservatism.

Model comparison and deployment decisions.

When you compare two models, do not just look at point metrics:

- Compare their entire uncertainty bands: are the differences statistically meaningful?
- Examine their tail behavior: does one model systematically expose you to worse drawdowns, even if average performance is similar?

When deploying an LLM-based forecasting system or transformer-driven signal engine, you want to understand not only whether it improves average performance but also how it reshapes the distribution of outcomes.

Summary: Thinking Like a Probabilistic Analyst

By now, you should see that probability and statistics are not abstract decorations; they are the language for reasoning about noisy, limited market data. The key habits to cultivate are:

- Treat returns and PnL as random draws from a distribution, not as deterministic outputs.
- Distinguish clearly between point estimates (mean, Sharpe, correlation) and the uncertainty around them.
- Use confidence intervals, sampling distributions, and bootstrapping to understand how noisy your performance metrics are.

- Guard against fooling yourself with multiple-testing, p-hacking, and regime blindness.
- Translate uncertainty into conservative risk limits and position sizing, rather than ignoring it.

With this probabilistic mindset in place, the more advanced modeling tools in later chapters—from classical time-series models to transformers and LLM-based market systems—become far more powerful. You will not only build models; you will know how much to trust them.

2.2 Linear Algebra, Calculus, and Optimization for Modeling

In the previous section, we adopted a probabilistic mindset: we treated returns and PnL as random variables, learned to work with expectations and variances, and began to quantify uncertainty. That gave us a way to judge *how much* we should trust a model.

In this section, we focus on *how* such models are built and trained. Modern ML systems, including transformers and LLM-powered market tools, rest on three mathematical pillars:

- Linear algebra, which provides the language of vectors, matrices, and high-dimensional geometry.
- Calculus, which describes how quantities change and how sensitive outputs are to inputs or parameters.
- Optimization, which uses gradients to adjust model parameters so that the model fits data or achieves a trading objective.

Our goal is not to turn you into a pure mathematician, but to make backpropagation, factor models, and training loops feel mechanical rather than mysterious. Each concept will be tied to concrete financial interpretations: positions, factor exposures, losses, and risk.

Vectors and Matrices as Financial Objects

You already think in vectors and matrices, even if you do not call them that. Any time you see a list or table of numbers, there is a linear-algebra structure hiding underneath.

Position vectors.

Imagine you trade N assets and hold a position in each: 100 shares of stock 1, short 50 shares of stock 2, and so on. You can collect these into a single *position vector*:

$$w = (\text{position in asset 1}, \dots, \text{position in asset N}).$$

Returns for the same assets on a given day form a *return vector*:

$$r = (\text{return of asset 1}, \dots, \text{return of asset N}).$$

The daily PnL of the whole portfolio is then essentially the *dot product* of the two:

$$\text{PnL} \approx w \cdot r.$$

You do not need formulas to get the idea: the portfolio PnL is the sum across assets of (position) $\times$ (return). That is a dot product.

Feature vectors.

In an ML context, the vector is usually a set of signals or features at a point in time. For example, for a single stock at time t you might define:

- Signal 1: 20-day momentum.
- Signal 2: earnings surprise.
- Signal 3: volatility.
- Signal 4: order flow imbalance.

Collecting them gives a feature vector x_t for that asset:

$$x_t = (\text{mom}, \ \text{earnings surprise}, \ \text{vol}, \ \text{order flow}).$$

A linear model that predicts next-day return is then given by another vector of parameters, β, and the predicted return is $\hat{y}_t = \beta \cdot x_t$. Again, a dot product.

Matrices: many vectors at once.

A matrix is just a grid of numbers. Two common examples in finance:

- **Covariance matrix:** rows and columns correspond to assets or factors; entries capture pairwise covariances. This matrix encodes how risks combine and diversify.
- **Feature matrix:** each row is an observation in time (or asset-time pair), and each column is a feature. When you feed data into an ML model, you are often feeding a matrix.

You can view matrix–vector multiplication as applying the same linear operation to many inputs. For example, if you apply a factor exposure matrix to a vector of factor returns, you obtain asset returns implied by your factor model.

Geometry in High Dimensions: Norms and Inner Products

Behind these dot products and matrices lies a simple geometric picture that generalizes familiar two-dimensional intuition.

Norms: measuring size.

A *norm* is a way to measure the size or length of a vector. The most common is the Euclidean norm, which corresponds to the usual distance notion: in two dimensions, it is precisely the length of the arrow from the origin to the point representing the vector.

In portfolio terms, the norm of a return vector over T days can be thought of as the overall volatility energy of that series. In feature space, the norm of a feature vector measures how "large" or "extreme" that observation is.

Inner products: measuring alignment.

The dot product $u \cdot v$ between two vectors u and v tells you how aligned they are:

- Large positive value: highly aligned (they point in similar directions).
- Near zero: mostly orthogonal (they do not move together).
- Large negative value: anti-aligned (point in opposite directions).

In finance:

- The dot product between two strategy return vectors over time reflects covariance and correlation; high alignment means they tend to win and lose together.
- The dot product between a factor exposure vector and a factor return vector gives the contribution to PnL from that factor.

Geometrically, when you regress returns on factors, you are projecting the return vector onto the subspace spanned by factor vectors. The residual is the part of returns that is orthogonal to (uncorrelated with) those factors.

Linear Transformations: Factors and Embeddings

A matrix can be seen as a machine that takes in a vector and outputs a new vector. This is a *linear transformation*. Many things you do in modeling are linear transformations in disguise.

Factor models as linear maps.

Consider a simple K-factor model. You have:

- A K-dimensional vector of factor returns f (for example, market, value, momentum).
- An $N \times K$ matrix of factor exposures B, where each row corresponds to an asset and each column to a factor.

Then the vector of predicted asset returns is $r_{pred} = Bf$. The matrix B is a linear transformation that maps factor-space returns into asset-space returns.

Embeddings and linear layers.

Later, when we use transformers on text or order books, we will encounter *embeddings*: representations of words, tokens, or states in a high-dimensional space. Every linear layer in a neural network is also just a matrix W that transforms an input vector x into Wx.

Once you are comfortable thinking of matrices as linear maps, many ML architectures reduce to stacking and composing such maps with simple nonlinearities in between.

Calculus as Sensitivity Analysis

Probability told us how to think about uncertainty in returns and metrics. Linear algebra gives us a way to organize data and model parameters. Calculus now ties them together by describing how changes in parameters affect model outputs and, ultimately, losses.

Functions as models.

You can think of a model as a function:

$$\text{prediction} = f(x; \theta),$$

where:

- x is an input vector (features, current state).
- θ is a parameter vector (weights of the model).
- f is the rule that maps inputs and parameters to a prediction (for example, a linear model, a neural network).

Training the model means choosing θ to make predictions match targets as well as possible.

Loss functions: turning performance into a single number.

To train systematically, we define a *loss function* $L(\theta)$ that measures how badly the model is doing across the dataset. Examples:

- Mean squared error between predicted and realized returns.

- Negative log-likelihood in a classification task (up/down direction).
- A differentiable approximation to a trading objective, such as maximizing risk-adjusted return while penalizing turnover.

The key is that $L(\theta)$ is a single number summarizing model performance for a given parameter vector θ.

Derivatives as local performance critiques.

In one dimension, the derivative of a function at a point tells you how fast the function is changing there. If we move a tiny step in the positive direction:

- Positive derivative: the function increases (loss gets worse).
- Negative derivative: the function decreases (loss improves).

In multiple dimensions, where θ is a vector, we use *partial derivatives*: one for each component of θ, holding the others fixed. Collecting all partial derivatives gives the *gradient*.

Gradients: Directions of Steepest Descent

The gradient of the loss with respect to parameters, often written $\nabla_\theta L$, is one of the most important objects in modern ML.

What a gradient tells you.

Think of the loss surface as a landscape in a high-dimensional parameter space:

- Each point on the landscape is a specific parameter choice θ.
- The height of the landscape at that point is the loss $L(\theta)$.

The gradient at a point is a vector pointing in the direction of steepest immediate increase of the loss. Its negative, $-\nabla_\theta L$, points in the direction of steepest immediate decrease.

So the gradient is a *local performance critique* of your parameters:

- If a particular parameter component has a large positive partial derivative, slightly increasing it will make the loss worse; you should move it down.
- If it has a large negative derivative, increasing it reduces loss; you should move it up.
- If the derivative is near zero, small changes to that parameter do not affect loss much locally.

Backpropagation as gradient bookkeeping.

In deep models, computing the gradient by hand would be messy. *Backpropagation* is an efficient algorithm that applies the chain rule of calculus repeatedly to compute the gradient of the loss with respect to all parameters in a network.

You do not need to work through the algebra manually. What matters is the conceptual picture:

- The model is a composition of simple operations (linear layers, activation functions).
- Each operation knows how to compute its contribution to the gradient.
- Backpropagation passes gradient information backward through the network, layer by layer, accumulating the effect on each parameter.

In practice, libraries such as PyTorch and JAX implement all of this via automatic differentiation. But understanding that the gradient is just a multi-dimensional derivative of the loss demystifies the process.

Curvature and the Hessian: Flat vs. Sharp Regions

The gradient tells you the direction of steepest change, but it does not tell you about the *shape* of the loss surface around you. For that, you need a sense of curvature.

Flat vs. steep directions.

In one dimension, curvature relates to whether a function is:

- Strongly curved (like a narrow bowl): small moves away from the minimum produce sharp increases in loss.
- Gently curved (like a wide, flat valley): you can move significantly without changing loss much.

In multiple dimensions, some directions can be steep while others are nearly flat. This anisotropy is summarized by the *Hessian*, the matrix of second derivatives.

You do not need to compute Hessians explicitly to appreciate the intuition:

- In steep directions, you must take small steps or you risk overshooting.
- In flat directions, you can take larger steps without destabilizing training.
- A very flat direction might indicate parameters or combinations that do not matter much, which is closely related to overparameterization and regularization.

Sharp minima and strategy brittleness.

In some regions, the loss surface may have sharp, narrow minima: small parameter changes dramatically worsen performance. In others, minima are wide and flat: many nearby parameter settings give similar performance.

Empirically, models that converge to flatter minima tend to be more robust out-of-sample. For trading, a sharp minimum can correspond to a brittle strategy whose performance depends on finely tuned parameters that are specific to the training sample; a flat minimum corresponds to a strategy that is less sensitive to small variations in the data or parameters.

From Geometry to Algorithms: Gradient-Based Optimization

Armed with gradients and basic curvature intuition, we can now discuss how models actually learn from data: by iteratively adjusting parameters to reduce loss.

Vanilla gradient descent.

The simplest algorithm is gradient descent:

- Start from an initial parameter vector θ_0.
- Repeatedly update:

  $$\theta_{k+1} = \theta_k - \eta \nabla_\theta L(\theta_k),$$

  where η is the *learning rate*, a small positive number.

Geometrically, at each step you move in the direction of the negative gradient—downhill on the loss surface. The learning rate controls the step size:

- Too large: you may overshoot minima, oscillate, or diverge.
- Too small: convergence is very slow; training may seem stuck.

Stochastic gradient descent (SGD).

In ML, datasets are large. Computing the exact gradient across all observations at each step is expensive. Instead, we approximate it by evaluating the gradient on a small random subset of the data (a "minibatch"). This yields *stochastic gradient descent*:

- It introduces noise into the gradient estimates, but this noise can help escape shallow local minima and saddle points.
- It allows training on massive datasets by streaming mini-batches.

In a trading context, SGD is analogous to learning from a subset of days or assets at a time, with the randomness averaging out over many updates.

Illustrating the Optimization Landscape

To make these ideas concrete, it is useful to visualize a two-dimensional loss surface, its gradients, and different optimization paths. Imagine a parameter vector $\theta = (\theta_1, \theta_2)$ and a loss function that is bowl-shaped but slightly skewed. Contour lines show levels of equal loss, gradients point perpendicular to contours in the direction of steepest ascent, and optimization paths trace how parameters move as training proceeds.

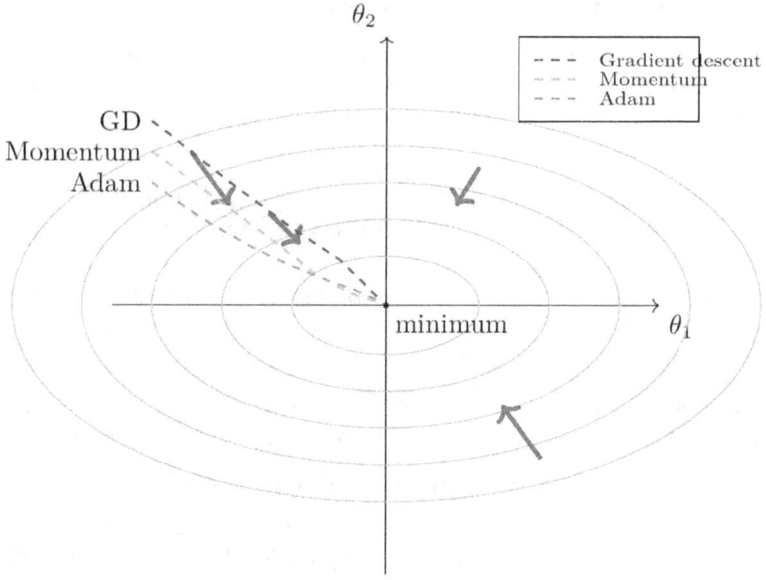

This diagram compresses several ideas:

- The contour lines are slices of equal loss: moving along a contour does not immediately change loss.
- Gradient vectors are perpendicular to contours and point toward higher loss; optimization moves in the opposite direction.
- Different optimizers trace different paths: basic gradient descent

zig-zags, momentum smooths the path, and Adam takes more adaptive, curved steps.

Momentum, Adaptive Methods, and Regularization

Building on plain gradient descent, modern optimizers introduce memory and adaptation to handle ill-conditioned and noisy landscapes.

Momentum: using past gradients.

Vanilla gradient descent only uses the current gradient. Momentum methods add a moving average of past gradients to the update. Intuitively:

- In directions where gradients repeatedly point in the same direction, the moving average builds up and accelerates progress.
- In directions where gradients oscillate, the moving average dampens the shaking, reducing zig-zagging.

In the loss surface picture, momentum transforms the path from a staircase pattern into a smoother, more direct trajectory along valleys.

Adaptive methods: scaling steps per parameter.

Algorithms like Adam go further: they adapt the effective learning rate for each parameter based on the magnitude of recent gradients. Parameters that consistently see large gradients get smaller steps; those with small gradients get relatively larger steps.

For complex models with many parameters of different scales, this adaptivity can dramatically speed up convergence and reduce the need for manual tuning.

Constraints and regularization.

Optimization always occurs within a modeling choice: are we searching over all possible parameter vectors, or only within some constrained region? In finance, constraints and regularization play two roles:

- **Risk control:** Limit gross leverage, sector exposures, or turnover via explicit constraints in the optimization problem.
- **Overfitting control:** Penalize large or complex parameter configurations so that the model favors simpler explanations unless the data strongly justify complexity.

Common regularization techniques include:

- L^2 (ridge) penalties, which discourage large parameter values and often produce smoother solutions.
- L^1 (lasso) penalties, which encourage sparsity and feature selection, paralleling the idea of focusing on a small number of robust signals.

Geometrically, regularization reshapes the loss surface or restricts the feasible region in parameter space, steering the optimizer away from extreme configurations that fit the training data too perfectly but generalize poorly.

Convex vs. Nonconvex Landscapes

The difficulty of optimization depends heavily on the shape of the loss surface.

Convex problems: no bad local minima.

A problem is convex if any line between two points in the feasible region lies entirely within the region and the loss function bends "upwards." In such problems:

- Any local minimum is also a global minimum.
- Gradient-based methods are guaranteed, under mild conditions, to converge to the global minimum.

Many classical portfolio optimization and linear regression problems are convex. This is one reason they are analytically tractable and numerically reliable.

Nonconvex problems: local minima and saddle points.

Neural networks and many practical trading objectives are nonconvex. Their loss surfaces have multiple valleys, plateaus, and saddle points:

- **Local minima:** Points where all nearby moves increase loss, but which are not the absolute best.
- **Saddle points:** Points where some directions are uphill and others are downhill.

Despite this theoretical complexity, experience shows that gradient-based methods often find good solutions in high-dimensional spaces, especially when aided by stochasticity (SGD), momentum, and good initialization.

For an autonomous analyst, the key is to understand that:

- Training a transformer or deep model means navigating a rugged loss landscape.
- Different runs (with different random seeds or data splits) can land in different minima with slightly different generalization behavior.
- Robust evaluation, as discussed in the previous section, is essential to separate genuine improvement from lucky landings in parameter space.

Connecting Back to Risk and Market Insight

Putting everything together:

- Linear algebra lets you represent portfolios, factor exposures, and embeddings as vectors and matrices, and to see risk and signal structure geometrically.
- Calculus provides gradients and curvature, turning performance gaps into precise directional feedback about how to adjust parameters.

- Optimization algorithms, from basic gradient descent to Adam, use this feedback to navigate the loss landscape and fit models to data.

For LLM- and transformer-based systems in markets, this framework carries over seamlessly:

- Token embeddings and hidden states are vectors in high-dimensional spaces.
- Attention layers are structured linear transformations.
- The training loop is gradient-based optimization of a loss that encodes predictive or generative quality, possibly enriched with financial objectives.

With these tools in hand, the next section on supervised learning and time-series models will show how to construct and evaluate concrete pipelines—from raw financial data to trained models—without treating the underlying math as a black box.

2.3 Supervised Learning and Classical Time-Series Models

So far, we have built two pillars. Probability and statistics taught us to treat PnL as random, to quantify uncertainty, and to avoid fooling ourselves with noisy backtests. Linear algebra and calculus showed that models are functions on vectors, trained by following gradients down a loss surface.

In this section, we put these ideas to work in a concrete workflow: an end-to-end supervised learning pipeline for financial time series. We will:

- Define supervised learning in trading terms.
- Lay out a pipeline from raw prices to trained models and backtest-style evaluation.

- Connect this pipeline to classical time-series models, such as AR and GARCH, as practical baselines.
- Highlight common pitfalls specific to financial ML: leakage, look-ahead bias, regime shifts, and overfitting.

By the end, you should have a clear mental template for how data, models, and evaluation fit together before you ever deploy transformers or LLM-based systems.

Supervised Learning in a Trading Context

Supervised learning is about learning a mapping from inputs to outputs, given example pairs.

- Inputs (*features* or *signals*): information you can observe at decision time (prices, volumes, news scores, factor values, order book statistics).
- Targets (*labels*): quantities you want to predict, defined in the future relative to the inputs (for example, next-day return, next-hour volatility, or a binary "up or down" indicator).

A few typical financial formulations:

- **Return regression:** predict next-period log-return of an asset or strategy.
- **Direction classification:** predict the sign of next return, "up" vs. "down," possibly with a "flat" class.
- **Volatility or risk forecasting:** predict realized volatility or Value-at-Risk over a horizon.

A supervised learning model is then a function

$$\hat{y}_t = f(x_t; \theta),$$

where x_t is the feature vector at time t, $\hat{y}_t$ is the model's prediction for the future target y_t, and θ are trainable parameters. Training chooses θ to make $\hat{y}_t$ as close as possible to y_t for past observations, according to a loss function.

From Raw Prices to a Modeling Dataset

Real data starts as messy time series of trades, quotes, and corporate events. To use supervised learning, you must convert this into a clean table of examples.

Step 1: Align and clean price data.

For a single asset or a universe:

- Synchronize prices to a regular grid (for example, daily closes or 5-minute bars).
- Adjust for corporate actions (splits, dividends) so that returns are meaningful.
- Handle missing data: decide how to treat days when an asset did not trade, was suspended, or has just IPO'ed.

The output is a time series P_t (or a panel $P_{i,t}$ for asset i at time t).

Step 2: Define targets.

Targets must always lie in the future relative to the features. Two common choices:

- *Next-period return:* $y_t = \log(P_{t+1}/P_t)$ for daily data, or the analogous multi-period return.
- *Direction label:* $y_t = 1$ if $y_t^{return} > 0$, and 0 otherwise.

For risk forecasting, the target might be realized volatility computed over a future window, such as the standard deviation of intraday returns over the next day.

Step 3: Build features that use only current and past information.

Features x_t may include:

- Price-based technicals: moving averages, momentum, mean-reversion indicators.

- Cross-sectional factors: valuation ratios, size, quality scores.
- Microstructure signals: spreads, order book depth, trade imbalance.
- Exogenous data: macro indicators, sentiment or news embeddings produced by an LLM.

The crucial rule is: at time t, x_t can depend on information up to time t, but not on any future P_{t+k}, events, or labels. Violating this leads directly to look-ahead bias.

Once you have (x_t, y_t) pairs for each time (and asset, if applicable), you stack them into a dataset. Rows represent observation-times, columns represent features, and an extra column holds the target.

Time-Aware Data Splitting: Train, Validation, Test

In generic ML, it is common to randomly shuffle data before splitting into training and test sets. For time series, this breaks causality and leaks future information into the past. In trading, splits must respect time.

Chronological splitting.

A typical pattern:

- **Training set:** an initial historical window (for example, 2008–2016).
- **Validation set:** the next window (for example, 2017–2018), used for model selection and hyperparameter tuning.
- **Test set:** a final window (for example, 2019–2021), held out until the end for an honest performance estimate.

Data from later years should never influence the training of models evaluated on earlier years.

Walk-forward and rolling schemes.

Markets evolve, so a single fixed split may be misleading. A more robust approach is walk-forward validation:

- Train on a window (for example, 2008–2014), validate on 2015.
- Roll the window forward: train on 2009–2015, validate on 2016, and so on.
- Aggregate performance across validation windows.

This mimics what you would have done in real time: periodically retrain on recent data and test on the immediate future.

Panel data and leakage across assets.

When you work with many assets, you also must watch for cross-sectional leakage. Examples:

- If features for stock A use an index that includes stock B, and you train a model on both, you must ensure that index computation uses only information available at the time.
- If you compute cross-sectional ranks each day (for example, ranking momentum), that is usually safe as long as ranks are based only on past prices, but ensure that ranks are computed within each day and do not inadvertently peek into the future of other assets.

The End-to-End Pipeline at a Glance

Before diving into specific models, it is useful to visualize the full supervised learning pipeline for financial time series.

Diagrammatic representation:

- Data preparation and feature engineering are as important as model choice.
- Time-aware splitting sits between features/targets and model training, acting as a guard against leakage.
- Backtest-style evaluation is the final consumer of model outputs, turning predictions into simulated trades, PnL, and risk metrics.

Model Families: From Linear to Nonlinear

With the pipeline in place, you can plug in different supervised learning models. Think of them as increasingly flexible function approximators.

Linear regression.

Linear regression assumes the target is a linear combination of features plus noise. In trading:

- It is easy to interpret: each coefficient tells you how sensitive the predicted return is to that feature.
- It is fast and stable when you have far fewer features than data points and when multicollinearity is moderate.
- It corresponds directly to a linear factor model if features are factors and targets are asset returns.

Linear regression is an excellent baseline: if a complex model cannot beat a well-regularized linear model out-of-sample, it is probably not learning stable structure.

Regularized linear models.

As you increase the number of features, plain linear regression becomes unstable and prone to overfitting. Regularization helps:

- L^2 (ridge) regression shrinks coefficients toward zero, reducing variance in estimates and improving generalization.
- L^1 (lasso) regression can set some coefficients exactly to zero, performing implicit feature selection.

In practice, you would tune the amount of regularization on the validation set, seeking a balance between bias and variance.

Tree-based models: decision trees, random forests, gradient boosting.

Trees split the feature space into regions and assign a prediction to each region. They can naturally capture:

- Nonlinear relationships (for example, a signal that only matters beyond a threshold).
- Interactions between features (for example, a combination of high volatility and low liquidity).

Tree ensembles, like random forests and gradient boosting, tend to be strong off-the-shelf performers. In finance, however, they must be used with care:

- They can fit noise in small datasets, so validation and walk-forward testing are crucial.
- They provide less transparent economic interpretation compared with linear models, although feature importance measures can help.

Simple neural networks.

Fully connected feed-forward networks (multi-layer perceptrons) extend linear models by stacking linear transformations with nonlinear activation functions. They offer:

- Flexibility to approximate complex relationships between features and targets.
- Capacity to integrate heterogeneous signals (for example, technical + fundamental + sentiment embeddings).

But they also:

- Require more data and careful regularization (dropout, weight decay).
- Are more sensitive to training choices (learning rates, initialization).

These same architectural ideas later scale up into transformers; understanding their basic behavior in time-series regression problems is good practice.

Metrics: How Do We Judge a Model?

The probabilistic mindset from earlier chapters is now applied to model evaluation.

Pointwise predictive metrics.

Depending on the task:

- For regression (predicting returns or volatility): mean squared error, mean absolute error.
- For classification (direction up/down): accuracy, precision, recall, F1 score, area under the ROC curve (AUC).

These metrics focus on how well predictions match targets on a per-example basis.

Trading-oriented metrics.

You ultimately care about what happens when you trade:

- Sharpe ratio and information ratio of the strategy that uses the model's predictions to size positions.
- Maximum drawdown, tail losses, and skewness of PnL.
- Turnover and transaction costs induced by acting on the model.

Proper evaluation translates predictions into a trading rule (for example, go long if predicted return exceeds a threshold, short if below another threshold), simulates trades over the test period, and computes these risk-return metrics with confidence intervals.

Uncertainty and robustness.

As in the earlier section, estimated performance is noisy:

- Two models may have similar Sharpe ratios, with overlapping confidence intervals; you should treat them as comparable rather than declaring a clear winner.

- Bootstrapping or repeated walk-forward splits can give a distribution of performance metrics, exposing sensitivity to start and end dates.

Supervised learning in finance is as much about robust evaluation as it is about model design.

Classical Time-Series Models as Baselines

Before jumping to complex ML, it is important to understand, and often deploy, classical univariate and multivariate time-series models. They are:

- More interpretable.
- Data-efficient.
- Good for sanity-checking and as benchmarks.

Autoregressive (AR) models.

An AR model predicts the current value of a series as a linear combination of its past values. For returns:

$$r_t = \phi_1 r_{t-1} + \phi_2 r_{t-2} + \cdots + \phi_p r_{t-p} + \epsilon_t,$$

where ϵ_t is noise.

Interpretation:

- AR(1) captures simple mean reversion or momentum: a positive ϕ_1 implies trend continuation; a negative ϕ_1 implies reversal.
- Higher-order AR models capture richer autocorrelation structures, such as weekly or monthly patterns.

Fitting an AR model is a form of supervised learning where the only features are lagged versions of the same series.

Moving average (MA) and ARMA/ARIMA models.

MA models express the series as a linear combination of past shocks (ϵ_{t-k}). ARMA combines AR and MA components; ARIMA extends ARMA to handle non-stationarity by differencing the series first.

Applications in finance:

- Modeling persistent drift and seasonality in macro variables or interest rates.
- Providing simple baselines for multistep-ahead forecasts.

ARIMA models force you to confront stationarity assumptions: are the mean and variance stable enough over time for the model to be meaningful?

Volatility models: GARCH.

Returns often show volatility clustering: periods of calm and turbulence. GARCH (Generalized Autoregressive Conditional Heteroskedasticity) models are designed to capture this:

- The return itself may be close to white noise.
- The conditional variance (volatility) follows its own autoregressive process, reacting to past squared returns and past variances.

For a trader, GARCH and its variants (EGARCH, GJR-GARCH) are useful baselines for volatility forecasting, Value-at-Risk estimation, and as building blocks in more complex risk models.

From classical to ML.

All of these classical models fit naturally into the supervised learning pipeline:

- Features: past values of the series (and possibly exogenous variables).
- Targets: current or future value or variance.
- Loss: typically squared error or likelihood-based.

Comparing a sophisticated ML model to a well-tuned AR or GARCH baseline is essential: if the complex model cannot beat these on honest out-of-sample tests, its added complexity is not justified.

Common Pitfalls in Financial ML

Financial ML differs from standard ML in several important ways. Ignoring these leads to models that backtest well but fail in production.

Look-ahead bias and label leakage.

This occurs when future information unintentionally contaminates features. Examples:

- Using end-of-day closing prices to form intraday signals, when in reality you would not know the close yet.
- Including post-earnings announcement drift signals that rely on data released after the prediction time.
- Using future realized volatility as a feature to predict returns at the same time.

Defensive practices:

- Explicitly document the information set available at each prediction time.
- Align timestamps carefully when merging datasets (prices, fundamentals, news).
- Simulate the actual data feed and delay structure you would have in production.

Overfitting and data snooping.

Financial series are noisy and often short. It is easy to:

- Test many signals and models until some appear to work by chance.
- Tune hyperparameters to squeeze extra Sharpe out of a backtest, which then disappears out-of-sample.

Mitigations:

- Use validation and test sets that are truly out-of-sample in time and, when possible, across markets or instruments.
- Penalize complexity: prefer simpler models and fewer features unless there is clear, repeated evidence they add value.
- Track the number of ideas and configurations you have tried; adjust your skepticism accordingly.

Regime shifts and non-stationarity.

Markets change. A model trained on one regime may break in another:

- Structural breaks: new regulations, market microstructure changes, or macro shocks.
- Slow drifts: evolving relationships between factors and returns.

Robust practices include:

- Testing models across multiple regimes: pre-crisis, crisis, recovery, low- and high-rate environments.
- Incorporating time-varying parameters or regime-switching components in models when appropriate.
- Monitoring live performance and being prepared to recalibrate or retire models as evidence accumulates.

Time Series as Sequences: Preparing for Transformers

Finally, it is helpful to reframe time series in a way that will later make transformers and sequence models feel natural.

Time as a sequence dimension.

A univariate time series can be viewed as a sentence of numbers:

$$r_1, r_2, r_3, \ldots, r_T.$$

A multivariate series (for example, multiple assets or multiple features) is like a sequence where each token is a vector, not just a scalar. In this view:

- Lagged values are past "words" that provide context for the current decision.
- Events (earnings, macro releases) and their text can be attached as annotations to positions in the sequence.

From fixed windows to flexible attention.

Classical models like AR and GARCH look back a fixed number of lags. Many ML pipelines also use fixed lookback windows to construct features. Transformers, in contrast, use attention mechanisms that can, in principle, weigh all past tokens when predicting the future.

To make effective use of transformers in markets, you must first master the basics covered here:

- How to build and evaluate honest supervised learning pipelines.
- How to compare complex models to robust classical baselines.
- How to encode time, regime, and event information in a way that respects causality.

Summary: A Reproducible Template

This section has developed a practical, end-to-end template for financial supervised learning:

- Start with raw, aligned price and market data; clean and adjust as needed.
- Define targets that lie strictly in the future of your features.
- Engineer features using only information available at decision time.
- Split data chronologically into train, validation, and test sets; consider walk-forward schemes.

- Train baseline models (linear, regularized, classical time-series) alongside more flexible ML models.
- Evaluate both predictive accuracy and trading performance with robust uncertainty quantification.
- Guard against leakage, overfitting, and regime shifts.

This pipeline is the backbone onto which we will later graft transformer architectures and LLM-based components. With it, your autonomous analyst will not just be powerful; it will be disciplined, testable, and grounded in sound quantitative practice.

Chapter 3

Transformer and LLM Fundamentals

Transformers are the engines behind today's most capable market copilots-but their power is easy to misuse if you treat them as black boxes. In this chapter we peel back just enough of the math and machinery to explain, in plain trading terms, how raw filings, news streams, and price tables become dense vectors; how attention lets models focus on the right clauses and patterns; and how pretraining, fine-tuning, and long-context tricks determine whether your "autonomous analyst" surfaces real insight or polished nonsense.

3.1 Tokenization, Embeddings, and Semantic Similarity

In the previous chapter we treated large language models (LLMs) at a high level: a black box that ingests text and produces predictions, summaries, or explanations useful to an analyst. In this section we open that box just enough to understand *how* raw financial information—filings, news, chat messages, and even tables—is converted into the numerical form a transformer can actually process.

The journey has three main stages:

- **Tokenization**: break raw text or table cells into small units called tokens and map them to integer IDs.
- **Embeddings**: map each token ID to a dense vector in a high-dimensional space (for example, 1,024 dimensions).
- **Semantic similarity**: compare these vectors (or aggregates of them) to find text that "means" roughly the same thing, even when phrasing differs.

This pipeline is the foundation of semantic search, clustering of analyst notes, retrieval of historical analogues, and deduplication of near-identical news. Once you understand it, you can design systems that use LLMs more efficiently and diagnose many failure modes that otherwise look mysterious.

From Raw Documents to Tokens

Transformers do not see words or characters directly. They see sequences of integers. Tokenization is the process that connects human-readable input to those integers.

Why we tokenize

Consider a short 10-K excerpt:

> Revenue increased 12% year-over-year, driven by strong growth in our cloud segment.

Feeding this string directly into a neural network would be inefficient and brittle. We want:

- A finite "vocabulary" the model can memorize during training.
- Reuse of sub-parts of words so that unseen words can still be understood.
- Stable handling of punctuation, numbers, and special symbols that are common in finance ("USD", "2027", "BBB-" etc.).

Tokenization addresses this by breaking the text into tokens and assigning each token a unique ID. The resulting sequence of IDs is what the model processes.

Subword tokenization in practice

Modern LLMs rarely operate at the level of whole words. Instead, they use *subword* tokenization schemes such as Byte Pair Encoding (BPE), WordPiece, or sentencepiece. These methods learn a vocabulary of character sequences that are:

- **Frequent enough** in the training corpus to be worth giving their own token.
- **Composable** so that rare or novel words can be built from a few tokens.

For example, a generic tokenizer might break

> "capitalization"

into tokens like:

> "capital", "ization"

or perhaps:

> "cap", "ital", "ization"

Even if the model has never seen the exact word "recapitalization" before, it will still recognize and interpret its pieces.

Finance-specific challenges

Financial language stretches generic tokenizers in several ways:

- **Tickers and identifiers**: "MSFT", "BRK.B", ISINs, CUSIPs, swap IDs, option symbols, and so on. A generic tokenizer may split "BRK.B" into "BRK", ".", "B" and treat each part separately.

- **Numbers**: Years (“2027”), prices (“102.375”), and ratios (“1.5x”) appear frequently but in many formats. Tokenizers might split “102.375” into “102”, “.”, “375”, or even smaller chunks.
- **Domain jargon**: Terms like “covenant-lite”, “basis risk”, or “macroprudential” may be decomposed oddly if they are rare in the model’s training mix.

None of this is fatal, but it affects both *quality* and *cost*. More tokens per document mean:

- Higher latency and compute cost (attention scales roughly with the square of sequence length).
- Increased chance that long filings will exceed the model’s context window.

Conversely, if the tokenizer is too coarse for your domain, the model may blur important distinctions (e.g., confusing similar tickers or failing to relate a table row to the corresponding textual disclosure).

Tokenizing tabular financial data

So far we have described plain text. But many critical signals live in tables: revenue breakdowns, maturity schedules, VaR reports, factor exposures.

There are two broad strategies for tables:

- **Linearize the table as text**. For example, a row in a maturity schedule might become:

  > “Maturity: 2027, Face value: 500 million USD, Coupon: 3.25 percent.”

  This is easy to feed into a standard tokenizer and LLM, at the cost of losing some layout structure.
- **Encode cells separately**. Each cell’s contents can be tokenized independently, sometimes with special separators to mark rows and columns. This is more complex, but preserves more of the table’s relational structure.

In both cases, the same tokenizer is usually applied: numbers, tickers, and labels are split into subwords and mapped to IDs. A table row thus becomes a short sequence of tokens, just like a sentence.

From Tokens to Embeddings

Once we have token IDs, the model transforms them into vectors. These vectors are called *embeddings*.

Token embeddings

Think of the embedding layer as a look-up table. For each token ID, the model stores a vector of, say, 1,024 real numbers. During inference:

- Each integer ID from the tokenizer indexes this table.
- The corresponding vector is retrieved.
- The sequence of token IDs becomes a sequence of vectors.

Geometrically, each token becomes a point in a very high-dimensional space. During pretraining, the model moves these points around so that:

- Tokens that appear in similar contexts end up close to each other.
- Tokens that rarely co-occur or signal different concepts are further apart.

For example, embeddings for "asset", "security", and "instrument" may cluster, while "asset" and "liability" may land in positions that reflect a structured relationship rather than simple similarity.

From tokens to span and document embeddings

In practice, analysts rarely work with individual token embeddings. We care about:

- A paragraph in a 10-K.
- A specific covenant clause.

- An entire news article.
- A row of a factor exposure table.

To obtain a single vector for a span of text (or a table row), we aggregate token-level information. There are multiple strategies:

- **Simple pooling**: average or sum the final-layer token embeddings across the span.
- **Special "[CLS]" or BOS token**: use a designated token whose embedding is trained to represent the whole sequence.
- **Dedicated embedding models**: feed the span to a smaller or specialized model that outputs a single vector directly optimized for similarity tasks.

In this chapter we will treat "embedding" of a span as a single vector that summarizes its meaning in a way that is useful for downstream tasks such as similarity search and clustering.

Visualizing the Journey to Embedding Space

The full pipeline can be visualized as a flow from raw data to points in a geometric space. We include a diagram here because having a clear mental picture will make the later, more abstract concepts easier to internalize.

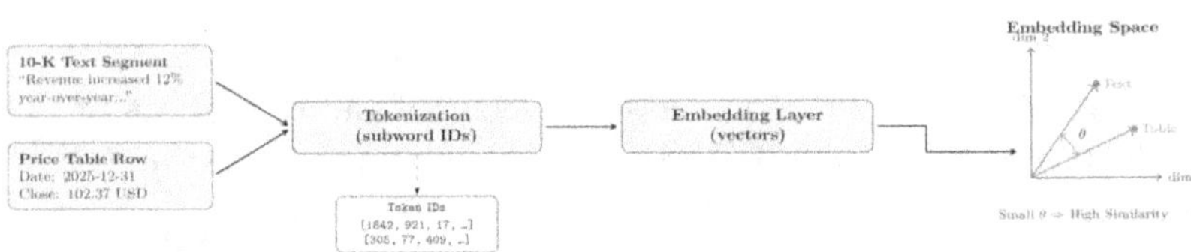

Semantic Geometry: Distances and Angles

Once text and tables are converted into vectors, we can compare them geometrically. The essential idea is that *semantic similarity corresponds to geometric closeness* in the embedding space.

Cosine similarity intuition

A common measure is *cosine similarity*. Given two vectors, we look at the angle between them:

- If the angle is small (vectors roughly point in the same direction), similarity is high.
- If the angle is large (vectors nearly opposite), similarity is low or even negative.

This is often more robust than directly comparing raw distances, because it focuses on *direction* rather than *length*.

For our purposes, you do not need the formula; it is enough to remember:

- Cosine similarity ranges from -1 (opposite) to 1 (identical direction).
- Values close to 1 mean the corresponding spans of text are semantically similar.
- We can use this measure to rank or cluster financial documents.

Why this works for market text

During pretraining, the model adjusts embeddings so that tokens and spans used in similar contexts are pulled closer together. For instance:

- Discussions of "liquidity risk" from two different banks may use very different wording, but they share patterns of co-occurrence (e.g., with "funding", "maturities", "committed facilities").
- Two descriptions of a similar rating downgrade—one from 2012 and one from 2024—might differ in phrasing but share structure: cause, impact, and outlook.

When we aggregate token embeddings into span or document embeddings, these contextual relationships carry over. As a result:

- Filings that describe similar business risks end up with similar embeddings.
- News articles about the same event, even if worded differently, land near each other.
- Table rows representing economically similar states (e.g., high leverage, low coverage) cluster.

This emergent geometry is what we exploit for search, clustering, and retrieval.

Practical Workflows Built on Embeddings

With this geometric intuition in mind, we can now connect embeddings to concrete workflows in a research or trading organization.

Semantic search over filings and research

Traditional keyword search matches surface strings. If you search for "supply chain disruption" you will miss filings that mention "logistics bottlenecks" or "manufacturing delays" if those exact words are absent.

Semantic search proceeds differently:

- Embed the user query into a vector.
- Embed candidate passages (e.g., paragraphs from 10-Ks, internal memos, or earnings call segments).
- Compute cosine similarity between the query vector and each passage vector.
- Return the top-k passages with highest similarity, possibly from across issuers and years.

This allows an analyst to ask conceptual questions like:

> "Find disclosures related to cyber risk incidents impacting operations."

and retrieve relevant passages even when the exact phrase "cyber risk" is not present, because the embedding captures related terms like "ransomware attack", "security breach", and "IT systems outage".

Implementation details that matter

To make this work well in finance:

- **Chunking**: Long documents must be split into overlapping chunks (e.g., 300–800 tokens). Each chunk receives its own embedding.
- **Domain coverage**: Generic embeddings from web-trained models may struggle with specialized topics (e.g., structured credit, local regulations). Finance-specialized embeddings, or at least mixed-domain training, can significantly improve relevance.
- **Indexing**: For large corpora (millions of chunks), approximate nearest-neighbor indices (e.g., HNSW graphs) are used to retrieve similar vectors efficiently.

Nearest-neighbor retrieval of historical analogues

Embedding similarity not only supports search; it enables pattern matching over time.

Suppose you are analyzing a new covenant in an issuer's bond indenture and you want to know:

> "Have we seen something like this before, and how did it play out?"

You can:

- Embed the new covenant clause.
- Compare it against an archive of previously embedded covenants and legal provisions.
- Retrieve the top neighbors—the most similar clauses historically.

- Inspect associated outcomes: realized losses, downgrades, litigation, etc.

This is an example of *nearest-neighbor retrieval*: using the geometry of the embedding space to find "look-alikes" from the past. A similar approach can be applied to:

- Management commentary in downturns vs. late-cycle phases.
- Crisis-era liquidity disclosures.
- Risk-factor language preceding large drawdowns.

By surfacing analogues, an LLM-driven system can provide context that goes beyond surface templates or single-keyword rules.

Clustering analyst notes and news

Clustering groups similar items without predefined labels. In embedding space, this reduces to:

- Compute embeddings for all items (e.g., daily research notes, broker reports, or incoming news headlines).
- Apply a clustering algorithm (k-means, hierarchical clustering, density-based methods).
- Inspect clusters to find themes or deduplicate redundant content.

In a research setting, clustering can:

- Reveal that many notes across desks are implicitly about the same macro theme (e.g., "higher-for-longer rates").
- Help prioritize reading by collapsing near-duplicate news wires into a single representative article.
- Organize a large internal library into more coherent topic groupings than a folder hierarchy can provide.

Because clusters are formed in semantic space, they reflect conceptual similarity rather than mere keyword overlap.

Deduplicating and normalizing news flows

Sell-side and news providers often blanket the same event with dozens of slightly varied headlines. Traditional deduplication via exact-text matching fails when:

- Headlines differ modestly ("Company X misses EPS" vs. "Company X profit falls short").
- Summaries are updated as more information appears.

Embedding-based deduplication works by:

- Embedding each incoming headline or short article.
- Maintaining an index of recent embeddings.
- For each new item, checking whether any existing item lies within a small distance threshold in embedding space.
- If such an item exists, flagging the new one as a near-duplicate, perhaps linking it to the canonical representative.

This reduces noise for human consumers and for downstream models that ingest news as features.

Choosing and Adapting Embeddings for Finance

Not all embeddings are created equal. When building systems in a financial context, you face several design choices.

General-purpose vs. finance-specialized embeddings

General-purpose embeddings (from web-trained models) have advantages:

- Broad coverage of everyday language.

- Good performance on many generic tasks (e.g., FAQ search, generic summarization).

However, they may:

- Underperform on specialized instruments, niche regulations, or local market jargon.
- Blur fine distinctions that matter in trading or risk management (e.g., subtle differences in covenant strength).

Finance-specialized embeddings incorporate financial text (filings, research, legal documents, regulatory guidance) more heavily in training. They tend to:

- Cluster domain-specific concepts more cleanly.
- Improve relevance for semantic search in filings or internal notes.
- Better align with practitioners' intuitive sense of "similarity" in financial language.

A pragmatic approach is often to start with a strong general-purpose model and monitor performance; for high-value workflows (e.g., credit committee preparation, regulatory capital models) you can migrate to finance-specialized embeddings when the marginal gain justifies the engineering cost.

Granularity: what gets an embedding?

Another design decision is the *unit* you embed:

- **Sentence-level**: suitable for fine-grained search and question answering over dense text.
- **Paragraph-level**: balances context and specificity; commonly used for filings.
- **Section-level or document-level**: good for clustering and thematic analysis.

- **Row-level for tables**: useful when each row represents a distinct economic observation (e.g., a trade, a position, a counterparty).

In practice, production systems often maintain multiple embedding granularities in parallel. For instance, a 10-K might be represented both as a collection of paragraph embeddings (for precise retrieval) and a single document embedding (for coarse clustering or similarity to other issuers).

Limitations and Failure Modes

Understanding where embeddings *struggle* is as important as knowing where they shine.

Sensitivity to tokenization choices

As discussed earlier, poor handling of tickers, long identifiers, or numerical formats can:

- Inflate token counts, raising cost and latency.
- Slightly distort semantic relationships (e.g., two syntactically similar but numerically different phrases may look more similar than they should).

If you observe systematic errors—for instance, the model grouping all maturity schedules together regardless of tenor—it is worth examining how those rows are tokenized and whether normalization (e.g., consistent number formatting) can help.

Hallucinated similarity

Embedding proximity does not guarantee economic equivalence. Two risk-factor disclosures may sound similar but refer to different underlying exposures. A model might:

- Overemphasize shared surface patterns (e.g., generic risk boilerplate).
- Underemphasize rare but critical distinctions (e.g., recourse vs. non-recourse exposure).

Therefore, semantic similarity should be treated as a strong *hint* rather than a final decision rule in risk-sensitive settings. Human review or additional structured features are often required for high-stakes use.

Temporal drift

Embeddings encode the statistical structure of the training data. Market language and institutions evolve:

- New products appear (e.g., crypto derivatives, ESG-linked loans).
- Regulatory regimes shift, changing the meaning or salience of certain disclosures.

Over time, a static embedding model may misrepresent or under-cluster emerging concepts. Periodic evaluation and, when appropriate, model refresh or adaptation are necessary.

Tokenization, embeddings, and semantic similarity form the base layer of LLM-based systems for market insight. Raw financial text and tables are first broken into tokens, which are mapped via an embedding layer into high-dimensional vectors. The geometry of these vectors—angles and distances—captures many aspects of semantic similarity that matter to practitioners: which disclosures resemble each other, which news stories are near-duplicates, and which historical events look like today's situation.

The rest of the chapter builds on this foundation. In the next section we will examine how transformers operate on these embeddings via attention, and how architectural choices (such as multi-head attention and positional encodings) affect the model's ability to track relationships across long and complex financial documents.

3.2 Attention Mechanics and Transformer Architecture

In the previous section we followed the journey from raw financial text and tables to embeddings: high-dimensional vectors that summarize the meaning of sentences, clauses, and rows. We now ask a deeper question: once a transformer has these vectors, *what does it actually do with them*?

This section focuses on the core engine of the transformer: *attention*. You will see how scaled dot-product attention, multi-head composition, and positional encodings work together to let an LLM:

- Decide which parts of a long sequence matter for each prediction.
- Track relationships between distant tokens in a 10-K or earnings call.
- Trade off capacity, latency, and context length in practical systems.

We will keep the mathematics light and emphasize intuitions anchored in familiar financial workflows: following references across an earnings call, tying a number in a table back to its narrative explanation, or relating a covenant clause to an earlier definition.

The Core Idea of Attention

At a high level, attention answers one recurring question:

> For this position in the sequence, which other positions are relevant, and how much should they matter?

Imagine you are listening to an earnings call. When the CFO says:

> "As mentioned earlier, our guidance for full-year 2026 assumes mid-single-digit volume growth in Europe."

To interpret "as mentioned earlier", you mentally scan back to the earlier guidance section. Your focus shifts to the exact numerical guidance and commentary you heard before. You *attend* to the relevant part of the sequence.

Attention in transformers works the same way, but with vectors:

- For each token (say, "guidance"), the model forms a view of "what I am looking for" in the rest of the sequence.
- It then scores how well every other token matches that query.
- These scores are turned into weights and used to mix information from the other tokens into a context-aware representation for the current position.

This mechanism is called *scaled dot-product attention.*

Scaled Dot-Product Attention: Queries, Keys, and Values

To describe scaled dot-product attention, we introduce three roles for each token embedding in a layer:

- **Query (Q)**: represents what this token is looking for.
- **Key (K)**: represents how this token can be matched or found by others.
- **Value (V)**: represents the information this token will contribute if it is attended to.

All three are just different linear projections of the same input embedding. Conceptually:

1. Start with the sequence of token embeddings (for example, a snippet from an earnings call transcript).
2. Pass each embedding through three small learned matrices to obtain Q, K, and V vectors.

Scoring relevance via dot products

For a given token position i (for example, the word "guidance"), attention computes how strongly it should attend to every position j (every other token in the call). The score between positions i and j is:

> the dot product between query Q_i and key K_j, appropriately scaled.

The dot product measures alignment:

- Large positive value: Q_i and K_j point in a similar direction in vector space; token j is highly relevant to token i.
- Small or negative value: token j is less relevant.

The "scaled" part (dividing by a factor related to vector dimension) keeps these scores numerically well-behaved, but the underlying idea is simply measuring similarity between queries and keys.

Turning scores into attention weights

Raw scores are turned into a set of weights using a softmax function. For each token i:

- All scores to other tokens j are exponentiated and normalized.
- We obtain weights that are positive and sum to 1 across all positions.

Intuitively, this is a soft selection:

- A few highly relevant tokens (for example, the original guidance figures) receive large weights.
- Many other tokens receive small but nonzero weights.

Finally, we construct a new representation for token i as a weighted sum of the *value* vectors V_j across the sequence, using these attention weights. This new vector for position i is now:

> a context-aware summary, emphasizing the positions that are most relevant to i.

Applied to an earnings call, this means:

- When the model processes a later reference to "our leverage target", attention can pull in information from earlier statements about specific leverage ratios, covenants, or balance sheet actions.
- When summarizing guidance, attention can gather details spread across multiple segments of the call: revenue growth, margin assumptions, and regional breakdowns.

A Layer-Level View with Positional Encodings

Before we go deeper into multi-head attention, it is useful to see how attention and positional encodings fit into the surrounding transformer block. Attention operates on *sets* of vectors, but the order of tokens in a financial document obviously matters: a "notwithstanding" clause can flip the meaning of everything that follows.

Transformers address this by adding *positional encodings* to token embeddings before attention. These might be fixed sinusoidal patterns or learned vectors that encode each position index.

Conceptually:

1. Start with token embeddings from the previous layer (or from the embedding layer for the first layer).
2. Add positional encodings to each token embedding so that the model can distinguish "first in the call" from "later in the call".
3. Feed the resulting position-aware embeddings into the attention module.

Right after we introduce attention conceptually, it is a good point to insert a visual summary.

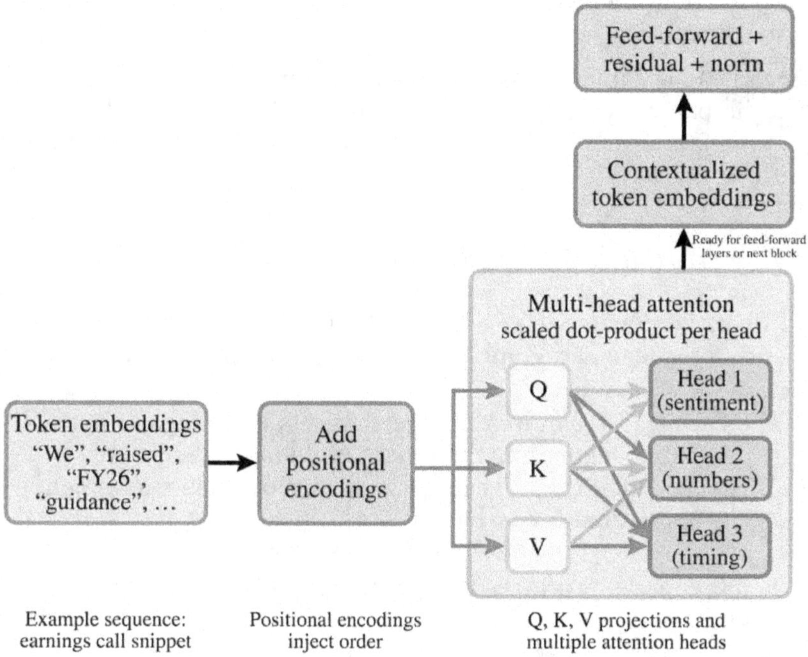

This figure shows one transformer block at a layer level: embeddings from the previous block enter on the left, positional information is added, multi-head attention computes context-aware representations, and a feed-forward sublayer (with residual and normalization) refines them before passing to the next block.

Multi-Head Attention: Looking in Many Ways at Once

So far we have described attention as if there were a single set of Q, K, and V projections. In reality, transformers use *multi-head attention*:

several attention mechanisms in parallel, each with its own Q, K, and V matrices.

Each head occupies a lower-dimensional subspace of the embedding, and its parameters are learned independently. After all heads compute their attention outputs, these outputs are concatenated and transformed again.

Why multiple heads?

In financial documents, a single notion of "relevance" is rarely sufficient. Consider a paragraph from a 10-K discussing a debt refinancing:

> "During the year, we refinanced $2.5 billion of senior notes due 2026, extending the weighted average maturity of our debt portfolio to 7.4 years and reducing our blended coupon by approximately 40 basis points."

When the model processes this paragraph, different types of relationships matter:

- **Temporal relationships**: linking "during the year" to "due 2026" and to the new maturity profile.
- **Quantitative relationships**: relating "$2.5 billion", "7.4 years", and "40 basis points".
- **Risk and impact**: connecting "refinanced" and "reducing coupon" to broader risk-factor language elsewhere.

Multi-head attention allows different heads to specialize:

- One head may learn to focus on numerical tokens and their nearby descriptors.
- Another may track causal phrasing ("due to", "as a result of").
- Another may attend across longer spans to follow cross-references ("as described under 'Liquidity and Capital Resources").

Each head thus offers a different viewpoint on the same sequence. Combining them yields a richer, more nuanced representation, which is especially valuable in long, jargon-heavy financial text.

Capacity and latency trade-offs

Multi-head attention also affects model capacity and computational cost:

- **Capacity**: More heads (with enough dimensionality per head) can capture more diverse patterns. Increasing the number of heads without increasing total embedding size often has diminishing returns, but moving from a single head to several is critical.
- **Latency**: Each head performs its own attention computation, though these can be implemented efficiently on modern hardware. Overall, attention scales roughly with the number of heads times the square of the sequence length.

For an *autonomous analyst* running over long bundles (10-K + 10-Q + press release + call transcript), these quadratic costs dominate latency. Later chapters will discuss efficient attention variants, but for now it is enough to recognize that:

> More heads and longer sequences increase both quality and cost; practical systems must strike a balance.

Positional Encodings: Recovering Order in Sets of Vectors

By design, attention treats its input as a set: it sums weighted values across the sequence without any built-in notion of order. Yet order is crucial in financial documents:

- The progression from historical performance to outlook in MD&A.

- The ordering of clauses in a covenant.
- The time axis in a time-stamped sequence of trades.

Absolute positional encodings

The simplest approach is *absolute* positional encodings:

- For each position index (0, 1, 2, ...) the model has a corresponding position vector.
- Before attention, this position vector is added to the token embedding.

The result is that two identical words appearing at different locations end up with slightly different embeddings. Attention can then use these differences to infer patterns related to position, such as:

- Tending to focus on nearby tokens (local context).
- Recognizing that certain sections (e.g., "Risk Factors") tend to appear earlier in the filing.

Sinusoidal positional encodings are a particular absolute scheme that use smooth, periodic functions of the position index; learned positional encodings instead allow the model to optimize these vectors directly.

Relative positional encodings

Absolute positions work well up to a point but do not generalize automatically when sequence lengths grow significantly, and they can be less convenient when you care about distances (*how far apart*) more than raw positions (*absolute index*).

Relative positional encodings address this by encoding the offset between tokens:

- Instead of asking "am I at position 512?", the model can represent "this token is 5 positions after that token".

- Attention scores are adjusted based on the relative distance, so heads can learn patterns like "prefer nearby tokens unless a cross-reference phrase is present".

For long financial documents, relative schemes are often more effective:

- They help the model generalize behaviors learned on shorter contexts to longer filings.
- They allow specific heads to specialize in short-range vs. long-range dependencies.

As context windows extend to tens or hundreds of thousands of tokens, the choice and implementation of positional encodings increasingly influences both quality and efficiency.

The Full Transformer Block

Attention is only one part of the transformer block. A standard block for an LLM used in finance contains:

1. **Layer normalization**: stabilizes the distribution of activations.
2. **Multi-head attention**: as described above, with residual (skip) connections.
3. **Feed-forward network (FFN)**: a small two-layer network applied independently to each position, again with residual connections.

The rough flow is:

1. Normalize inputs from the previous layer.
2. Apply multi-head attention (with positional encodings already added).

3. Add the attention output back to the input via a residual connection.
4. Normalize again and pass through the feed-forward network.
5. Add this FFN output back to form the block output.

Why residual connections and FFNs matter

Residual connections allow information to flow more easily through many stacked layers, which is essential for deep transformers that must reason across hundreds of pages.

Feed-forward networks add non-linear transformations at each position, helping the model:

- Compress, expand, or reweight the information gathered by attention.
- Implement complex token-wise transformations, such as mapping from a raw number token and its context to a more abstract representation of "high leverage" or "negative free cash flow".

In combination, attention plus FFN layers form a powerful building block. Stacking many such blocks gives the model depth: the ability to successively refine representations from near-surface text patterns to more abstract concepts like business models, risk structures, and macro sensitivities.

Sequence Length, Quadratic Cost, and Long Financial Documents

A critical practical issue for market applications is how attention cost scales with sequence length. For each head, attention requires computing relevance scores between all pairs of positions in the sequence. If there are N tokens:

- The attention matrix is $N \times N$.

- Computation and memory grow roughly with N^2.

This has direct consequences:

- Doubling the number of tokens in a context (say, from a 50-page to a 100-page bundle) roughly quadruples the attention cost.
- Very long sequences—full corporate histories, multi-year call archives—become expensive to process with naive attention.

Impact on an autonomous analyst

For an autonomous analyst, context length determines how much material can be considered at once:

- A shorter context may force aggressive truncation or chunking of filings, risking loss of important cross-references.
- A longer context allows richer reasoning across documents (linking footnotes in 10-Ks with risk-factor changes and call commentary) but increases latency and compute cost.

Architectural choices—including attention variants, sparse patterns, or external retrieval mechanisms—are therefore not just academic details. They materially affect:

- The scale of document bundles you can process.
- The responsiveness of interactive analyst tools.
- The feasibility of running models frequently in production systems.

We will revisit these issues when we discuss long-context modeling and retrieval-augmented generation in later sections. For now, you should remember:

> Attention is powerful because every token can, in principle, look at every other token; it is expensive for the same reason.

Attention and transformer architecture provide the machinery that turns static embeddings into dynamic, context-aware representations:

- **Scaled dot-product attention** lets each token, at each layer, selectively gather information from the entire sequence based on learned notions of relevance.
- **Multi-head attention** gives the model multiple specialized "views"—tracking numbers, sentiment, temporal references, and more—crucial for understanding complex financial language.
- **Positional encodings** restore order information, enabling the model to distinguish earlier from later disclosures and to reason about local and long-range dependencies in long documents.
- **The full transformer block** combines attention, feed-forward transformations, normalization, and residual connections to build deep models that can track intricate relationships across filings, news, and internal research.

These architectural choices directly shape model capacity, latency, and context length. Understanding them equips you to design and operate LLM systems that balance depth of insight with practical constraints when deployed as autonomous or semi-autonomous analysts in real financial workflows.

3.3 Pretraining, Fine-Tuning, and Long-Context Modeling

The previous sections treated transformers as fixed engines: you saw how tokenization produces embeddings, and how attention layers rearrange information across long sequences of financial text. In practice, however, the behavior you observe when you query an LLM as an "autonomous analyst" is largely determined by *how it was trained* and *what it saw* during that training.

This section connects those training choices to the model's downstream behavior in markets. We will move in three steps:

1. Large-scale **pretraining**: how objectives like next-token prediction, together with the composition of the training corpus, shape the model's prior beliefs about language, institutions, and markets.

2. Task-specific **fine-tuning and alignment**: how curated supervision and preference feedback adapt a general model into a more cautious, controllable assistant for finance.

3. **Long-context and multimodal modeling**: how architectural strategies such as efficient attention, retrieval, and hierarchical processing extend LLMs to hundreds of pages of filings, multi-document reasoning, and text-plus-tables analysis.

Throughout, we focus on design decisions that an investment or risk team must make when deploying LLMs in production.

Pretraining: How the Model Learns to Talk and Reason

Pretraining is the phase where the model becomes broadly capable: it learns syntax, common knowledge, and many statistical regularities of the world. This phase typically dominates the computational budget.

Next-token prediction as the core objective

Most modern LLMs are trained with some variant of *next-token prediction*. The setup is simple:

- Feed the model a long sequence of tokens (for example: "In the third quarter of 2022, the company reported net income of").

- Ask it to predict the next token ("$", "153", "million", etc.).

- Compare its predicted probability distribution over tokens with the true token that follows.

- Adjust the model's parameters slightly to increase the probability of the correct token.

Repeated billions or trillions of times, over many documents, this objective encourages the model to:

- Capture grammar and style (how sentences are typically formed).
- Learn factual associations ("dividends are usually paid in cash or stock", "10-K is an annual SEC filing").
- Internalize patterns in narrative structure, such as how earnings releases progress from headline numbers to segment breakdowns and outlook.

From the standpoint of a finance practitioner, next-token prediction has two crucial implications:

1. It rewards *fluency*: the model becomes very good at continuing text in a way that *sounds* right.
2. It does not inherently reward *truth*: if the training data contains inconsistent or noisy statements, the model learns their patterns as they appear, without a built-in concept of factual correctness.

This explains why even very strong models can occasionally hallucinate details about niche instruments or regulations they have rarely seen.

Masked language modeling and other variants

Some models, especially earlier transformer-based language models, also use *masked language modeling*. Here, a portion of the input tokens is randomly hidden, and the model is trained to reconstruct the missing pieces from the surrounding context.

Masked objectives place more emphasis on understanding bidirectional context—what comes both before and after a token—whereas pure next-token prediction is typically left-to-right. Many modern systems use hybrids or related objectives, but the underlying idea is similar: learn a compressed representation of language that makes local predictions accurate.

For market applications, the precise mix of objectives is less important than understanding that:

- The model learns to be a strong pattern recognizer and generator.
- Its notion of "meaning" is tied to statistical co-occurrence, not to an external database of ground truth.

Data mixtures: what the model reads

Equally important is *what* the model reads during pretraining. A typical large model is exposed to a mixture of:

- General web text (articles, forums, blogs).
- Books and encyclopedic content.
- Code.
- News and possibly some public filings or financial commentary.

The exact mixture is rarely public, but the qualitative impact is clear:

- Heavy exposure to general web and books yields strong everyday language skills and broad world knowledge.
- Exposure to code improves logical structure, precision, and the ability to follow algorithmic instructions.
- Limited direct exposure to specialized financial documents means that niche jargon, local regulations, and rare instruments may be underrepresented or approximated from related text.

From the perspective of an autonomous analyst:

- The model is often excellent at "financial English"—it understands MD&A narratives, news reports, and broker-style prose.
- It may be less reliable on idiosyncratic details: a bespoke swap schedule, a tiny local exchange, or a newly introduced reporting standard.

The pretraining mixture thus defines the model's *priors*: its default expectations about how companies, markets, and institutions behave.

Hallucinations and domain gaps

Because pretraining optimizes for predictive likelihood on its corpus, not for real-world accuracy, the model may:

- Fill in plausible-sounding but incorrect numbers in a balance sheet table if you ask it to "reconstruct" one.
- Invent regulatory clauses that resemble those in other jurisdictions but do not exist in the one you care about.

These behaviors are not bugs in the training process; they are natural consequences of the objective. Mitigating them requires:

- Careful *prompt design* and system-level safeguards.
- *Fine-tuning and alignment*, which we discuss next.
- External *retrieval* from trusted sources when precise facts matter.

Fine-Tuning: Shaping the Model for Financial Tasks

Once a model has been pretrained, it can be further adapted to specific tasks and domains. This stage is often where a generic language model becomes a useful financial co-pilot.

Supervised fine-tuning on curated datasets

In supervised fine-tuning (SFT), the model is trained on labeled examples that reflect the behaviors you want:

- Question-answer pairs over 10-Ks (e.g., "What were the main drivers of margin compression in FY2023?" $\rightarrow$ answer pointing to relevant sections).
- Rating-action rationales (e.g., a text description of the reasons for a downgrade, labeled by analysts).

- Chain-of-thought explanations of macro events (step-by-step rationales connecting data releases, policy moves, and asset price reactions).
- Classification labels (e.g., whether a disclosure reflects increasing or decreasing liquidity risk).

During SFT, the loss function directly rewards the model for producing outputs close to the human-provided answers or rationales. This:

- Aligns the model's style with house standards (tone, level of detail, structure of reasoning).
- Reduces idiosyncratic hallucinations in well-covered domains by consistently exposing the model to correct answers for common patterns.
- Encourages the model to surface relevant parts of the input (for example, citing specific passages in a filing).

For a firm building an in-house autonomous analyst, constructing such datasets is akin to building a high-quality internal research library, but labeled and structured for machine consumption.

Adapters and parameter-efficient tuning

Full fine-tuning of all model parameters can be expensive and operationally complex. An increasingly popular alternative is *parameter-efficient* tuning, where:

- Small adapter modules (such as low-rank updates or lightweight feed-forward layers) are inserted into the transformer.
- Only these adapters are trained on domain-specific data; the base model weights remain frozen.

This approach:

- Reduces computational cost and hardware requirements.
- Allows multiple domain-specific adapters (e.g., credit, macro, commodities) to coexist on top of a common base model.

- Simplifies upgrades: as new base models become available, adapters can be re-evaluated or transplanted with minimal retraining.

For many finance teams, adapter-based tuning strikes a practical balance between customization and maintainability.

Alignment and Instruction-Tuning: Making the Model Safe and Controllable

A model that is merely pretrained and SFT-tuned may still behave in ways that are undesirable in a risk-sensitive environment. It may:

- Overstate its confidence in ambiguous situations.
- Provide speculative or inappropriate recommendations.
- Fail to say "I do not know" even when it should.

Instruction-tuning: learning to follow directions

Instruction-tuning exposes the model to many examples of natural-language instructions paired with appropriate responses. In a financial context, these instructions might include:

- "Summarize the key sources of liquidity risk in the following disclosure."
- "Compare management's tone in the latest call to the previous quarter in three bullet points."
- "Explain this rating downgrade to a non-technical investor, avoiding jargon."

The model learns not just factual mappings, but also the *shape* of good responses: concise, structured, and relevant.

Reinforcement learning from human or preference feedback

To further refine behavior, many systems use *reinforcement learning from human feedback* (RLHF) or closely related preference-optimization methods. The process is conceptually:

1. Collect pairs of candidate answers from the model for the same prompt.
2. Ask human reviewers (for finance, typically domain experts) which answer is better and why.
3. Train a separate "reward model" to predict these preferences.
4. Optimize the base model so that, under this reward model, it tends to produce higher-rated answers.

In a financial setting, reviewers can reward answers that:

- Are cautious about uncertain claims.
- Explicitly acknowledge missing data or limitations.
- Distinguish clearly between historical facts, model-based projections, and speculative scenarios.
- Respect compliance and regulatory constraints (for example, avoiding personalized investment advice where it is not permitted).

Alignment thus moves the model closer to being a reliable collaborator rather than a mere text generator.

Long-Context Modeling: From Paragraphs to Hundreds of Pages

So far we have considered how objectives and supervision shape the *behavior* of the model. The next question is: *how do we scale that behavior to long financial artifacts?*

Annual reports, multi-year call archives, and cross-issuer comp sets can easily exceed hundreds or thousands of pages. Naively feeding all tokens into a standard transformer is often infeasible because of the quadratic cost of attention.

Several complementary strategies address this challenge.

Efficient attention variants and sparse patterns

One direction is architectural: modify the attention mechanism to reduce cost. Examples (at a conceptual level) include:

- **Local attention**: each token attends primarily to nearby neighbors; only some layers or heads look globally. This is effective when most dependencies are local, as in many narrative sections of filings.
- **Sparse or block attention**: the sequence is divided into blocks (for example, per section), with attention primarily within blocks and limited cross-block links. This mirrors how humans often read: focusing on one section at a time, with occasional cross-references.
- **Low-rank or kernelized attention**: approximate the full attention matrix with a more compact representation, reducing complexity from quadratic toward linear in sequence length.

These variants allow context windows to grow from tens of thousands to hundreds of thousands of tokens at a manageable cost, at the expense of some flexibility in which tokens can attend to which others.

For an autonomous analyst, such architectures support workflows like:

- Ingesting an entire 10-K plus prior-year filings in a single pass.
- Maintaining awareness of earlier risk-factor language while reading the latest MD&A.

Recurrent memory and segment-level state

Another strategy is to process long documents in segments while carrying a compressed *memory* state forward. Conceptually:

- The model reads the first chunk of the filing, producing both token-level outputs and a summary state.
- This summary state is fed, along with the next chunk, into the model.
- The process repeats, with the memory accumulating knowledge about the document.

This resembles how an analyst retains key points in working memory while reading. It reduces the need to keep the entire token sequence explicitly in the attention window, while still allowing earlier context to influence later reasoning.

Retrieval-Augmented Generation (RAG)

Perhaps the most practical and widely adopted strategy is *retrieval-augmented generation.* Instead of expecting the model to hold an entire corpus in its short-term context, you:

1. Pre-compute embeddings for document chunks (paragraphs, sections, table rows) across your corpus.
2. Store them in a vector index optimized for nearest-neighbor search.
3. When a user poses a query or task, embed the query and retrieve the most relevant chunks.
4. Construct a prompt that includes the user's question and the retrieved chunks.
5. Ask the LLM to answer or analyze, *grounded* in this retrieved evidence.

RAG leverages the semantic similarity machinery introduced earlier in the chapter. It transforms long-horizon tasks such as:

- "Compare how Company A has described cyber risk over the last five years."
- "Identify changes in non-GAAP metrics definitions across three reporting periods."

into a sequence of shorter-context problems, each supported by a curated subset of the corpus. The base model's context window still matters, but retrieval effectively stretches its reach across much larger datasets.

Hierarchical chunking and summarization

In truly large-scale settings—say, aggregating information from hundreds of issuers across decades—one often adopts *hierarchical* strategies:

- At the lowest level, the model reads small chunks (paragraphs, rows) and produces local summaries or tags.
- These are then synthesized into section-level or document-level summaries.
- Higher-level modules operate on these summaries to perform cross-document comparison, clustering, or portfolio-level analysis.

This hierarchy mirrors how human analysts work: they do not hold all raw text in mind simultaneously, but progressively abstract and compress it into mental models.

Multimodal Extensions: Text, Tables, and Charts

Financial analysis is inherently multimodal: beyond text, you rely on numbers in tables, time series charts, factor loadings, and even geospatial data. Extending LLMs to these modalities involves both architectural and training changes.

Tables and structured data

For tables and structured data, there are two main patterns:

- **Textual linearization**: convert each row or cell into a structured textual description that can be processed by a standard language model.
- **Tabular encoders**: use specialized encoders that understand rows, columns, and sometimes relational structure, then feed their outputs into or alongside the language model's text embeddings.

Training objectives may include predicting masked cells, classifying anomalies, or answering questions that require joint reasoning over text and tables (for example, "Is the disclosed liquidity position consistent with the maturity schedule?").

Charts, images, and other modalities

When models incorporate visual encoders, they can ingest:

- Line charts of price or volume.
- Bar charts of segment revenue.
- Images of slides from investor presentations.

A vision encoder maps these inputs into vectors that can be fused with text embeddings through attention. Pretraining may involve objectives such as:

- Predicting captions from images.
- Matching tables or charts to their surrounding narrative.

For an autonomous analyst, multimodality enables more natural workflows: you can paste a slide from an earnings deck and ask the model to relate it to textual disclosures, or to reconcile a chart with time series data in your own database.

Designing Training and Adaptation for Market Use

Bringing these elements together, an organization designing LLM systems for market insight must make several strategic choices:

- **Base model selection**: choose a pretrained model whose data mixture and capabilities broadly match your needs.
- **Domain adaptation**: decide whether to use generic embeddings and prompts with retrieval, to fine-tune with domain-specific text, or to train adapters for critical verticals (credit, macro, quant research).
- **Alignment strategy**: define reward signals that encode your risk culture—how cautious the model should be, how to handle uncertainty, what explanations should look like.

- **Context strategy**: combine long-context architectures, retrieval, and hierarchical summarization to cover the scale of data you care about without incurring prohibitive cost.
- **Evaluation and monitoring**: treat the model as an evolving analyst whose performance you must measure over time, across tasks and regimes, adjusting training and retrieval pipelines as needed.

Pretraining, fine-tuning, and long-context modeling determine how a transformer-based system behaves when you ask it to act as an autonomous analyst:

- Pretraining on massive corpora imbues the model with broad language competence and general market priors but does not guarantee factual accuracy on niche topics.
- Fine-tuning and alignment, using curated financial datasets and expert feedback, shape the model's style, caution, and task performance so it behaves more like a disciplined junior analyst than a free-form text generator.
- Long-context and multimodal modeling, through efficient attention, memory, retrieval, and specialized encoders, extend the model from single paragraphs to entire research libraries and from pure text to tables and charts.

In the chapters that follow, we will build on this foundation to design full systems: pipelines that combine LLMs, retrieval, evaluation, and integration with existing data infrastructure to create robust, auditable tools for trading, risk, and investment research.

Chapter 4

Data Engineering for Retrieval-Augmented Finance

Most attempts to build "AI for markets" fail long before the model is trained: they collapse under messy schemas, silent data drift, and unverifiable history. This chapter shows how to flip that script-treating data engineering as a first-class trading edge. You will learn to design pipelines where every number is time-stamped, explainable, and replayable, so your retrieval-augmented LLMs sit on top of a living, auditable record of the market-rather than a pile of spreadsheets and hope.

4.1 Ingestion, Quality, and Lineage Pipelines

In the previous chapters we treated "market data" and "documents" as if they were simply *there*: time series of prices, fundamental indicators, and neatly chunked filings, all ready to be retrieved and fed into an LLM-powered analyst. In real trading organizations, that neat picture is an illusion. Behind every apparently simple query like "what was Apple's market cap on the day before its last 10-K?" there is a surprisingly intricate data-engineering machine.

This section opens that black box. We will walk through the end-to-end flow of financial data from raw sources into governed, point-in-time stores, and explain how three ideas—*data contracts*, *validation*, and *lineage*—form the non-negotiable foundation for any credible LLM or analytics layer.

From Raw Feeds to Governed Stores: The Big Picture

At a high level, a retrieval-augmented finance system must do four things with data before an LLM or model can safely use it:

1. **Ingest** it from messy, heterogeneous sources in a way that preserves the original information.

2. **Normalize and transform** it into a coherent schema (symbols, currencies, calendars, time zones, corporate actions).

3. **Check and enforce quality** continuously, with explicit expectations instead of ad-hoc "sanity checks."

4. **Track lineage** so that every derived value can be traced back to specific inputs and transformations.

LLMs amplify both insight and error. If a price series has survivorship bias, or a fundamental feature quietly incorporates future restatements, a traditional factor backtest is already in trouble. Add an LLM that confidently explains those biased results, and you have an extremely persuasive *but wrong* story. That is why the data plumbing matters at least as much as clever prompt engineering.

Right after this conceptual orientation, it is helpful to anchor the discussion with a visual overview of the architecture.

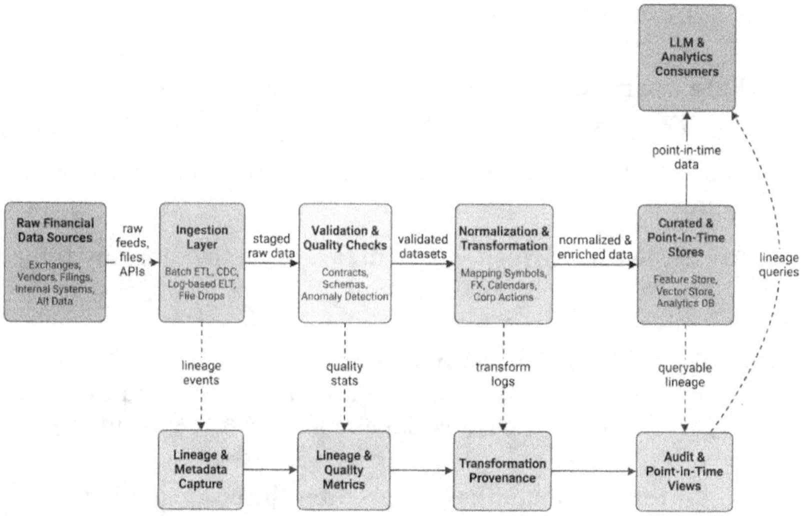

This layered diagram illustrates the architecture we will develop: raw data flowing left to right through ingestion, validation, and transformation into curated, point-in-time stores; metadata and lineage captured in a parallel lane and exposed to LLM and analytics consumers.

Understanding Financial Data Sources and Their Quirks

Before we talk about pipelines, we must understand what actually flows through them. Financial data is not one monolithic category; it comes from several distinct kinds of sources, each with behaviors that shape your ingestion design.

Exchange and vendor data.
This includes trades, quotes, order book updates, and end-of-day bars, as well as reference data such as symbol masters and corporate actions. Typical quirks:

- **Late corrections** (e.g., a trade initially reported at the wrong price).
- **Different calendars and time zones** (US equity vs. FX vs. futures).
- **Multiple identifiers** (different tickers for the same instrument across vendors, plus internal IDs).

Fundamental and regulatory data.
Filings (10-K, 10-Q, 20-F), earnings announcements, and fundamentals (revenues, earnings, balance sheets) have their own quirks:

- **Restatements** months or years after the original filing.
- **Multiple dates per record**: period end date, filing date, acceptance date.
- **Sparse and irregular timing**, unlike clock-like price data.

Internal trade, risk, and P&L systems.
These capture your own positions, trades, risk measures, and limits. Their quirks:

- **System-specific schemas and conventions** that may not match external data.
- **End-of-day batch runs** that recompute measures, sometimes changing history due to bug fixes or methodology changes.

Alternative datasets.
Think of web-scraped data, satellite imagery metrics, credit card panel data, or sentiment feeds:

- **Unstructured or semi-structured formats**: JSON logs, images, text.
- **Uncertain coverage and bias**: some issuers or regions are systematically missing.
- **Evolving definitions**: a "sentiment score" from one year may not be comparable to the same field later.

A robust ingestion architecture respects these quirks. Instead of flattening everything into a "one-size-fits-all" table, it preserves the raw form and semantics, then progressively normalizes and aligns data for downstream use.

Ingestion Patterns: Bringing Data into Your Environment

"Ingestion" is the process by which data crosses the boundary between external sources (vendors, exchanges, web) and your internal environment (data lake, warehouse, or lakehouse).

Four practical ingestion patterns cover most scenarios:

Batch ETL (Extract-Transform-Load).
Traditional vendors deliver daily files via SFTP or object storage. A batch ETL pipeline might:

1. Download the file to a landing area.
2. Parse and validate each record.
3. Transform data into your canonical schema.
4. Load into curated tables.

ETL emphasizes transformation *before* loading. It works well when schemas are stable and volumes are manageable (for example, daily fundamental snapshots).

ELT and log-based ingestion.
With modern cloud storage, it is often safer to ingest first and transform later (ELT: Extract-Load-Transform):

1. Ingest raw data into an immutable "bronze" or "raw" zone as-is.

2. Apply transformations downstream to produce "silver" (clean) and "gold" (curated) layers.

Log-based ingestion, such as capturing a vendor feed or database change data capture (CDC) stream into an append-only log (Kafka, Kinesis, Pulsar), is especially powerful for time-sensitive data, because you keep the original order of events and can replay history as needed.

Change Data Capture (CDC).
CDC tracks inserts, updates, and deletes in a source database and publishes them as ordered events. For internal trading or risk systems, CDC has two advantages:

- You avoid heavy full-table extracts every night.

- You retain a fine-grained history of how records evolved, essential for point-in-time reconstruction.

File-drop ingestion.
Alternative data providers often place new files into an object store location when ready. A simple ingestion subsystem watches for new files, then moves them through validation and processing. Even this apparently simple pattern benefits from explicit contracts and lineage: which provider, which version of the extraction logic, which coverage period?

Across these patterns, the golden rule is: *never throw away the raw data.* Store it immutably (with timestamps and source identifiers) so that future analysts—and future you—can understand and fix mistakes without guessing what the source looked like.

Schema Design and Normalization: Creating a Coherent Market View

Once data is ingested, you must make heterogeneous feeds look coherent enough that downstream models and LLMs can ask intelligible questions. This is the role of schema design and normalization.

Key normalization dimensions in finance include:

Instruments and identifiers.
The same economic instrument might appear as “AAPL,” “US0378331005” (ISIN), “037833100” (CUSIP), or a proprietary internal key. Your schema should:

- Maintain a **master instrument table** linking all identifiers.
- Track **lifetimes** of symbols to handle ticker changes and reuse.
- Distinguish **issuer** (company) from **security** (specific share class or bond).

Currencies and units.
Prices, notional amounts, and fundamentals appear in many currencies and unit conventions. A well-designed schema:

- Stores the *original* currency and unit alongside any converted values.
- Records which FX rate source and timestamp were used for conversions.

Calendars and time zones.
An LLM query like “what was the closing price before the earnings announcement?” only makes sense if dates and times are aligned:

- Store timestamps in a consistent base (often UTC), with explicit original time zone.
- Model **trading calendars** for each venue (trading days, holidays, early closes).
- Attach both *event time* (when something happened on the exchange) and *processing time* (when you ingested or computed it).

Corporate actions.
Splits, dividends, and mergers can drastically alter price and volume series. You should:

- Store corporate actions as first-class entities, not as mere adjustment factors.
- Keep both **raw** and **adjusted** price series, with clear flags indicating which one you are using in any analysis.

The goal is not to force every dataset into a single monolithic table. Rather, it is to define a set of shared keys and conventions that make joins and cross-source comparisons meaningful and reproducible. When an LLM retrieves both a price series and a filing for a given issuer around a given date, those items should align because the data model makes such alignment natural.

Data Contracts: Making Expectations Explicit

Data contracts formalize the relationship between data producers (vendors, internal systems) and consumers (quant researchers, LLM services, risk reports). Informally, a contract answers the question: *"What exactly may I assume about this dataset?"*

A practical data contract for a table or topic specifies at least:

- **Schema**: field names, types, allowed values or enumerations.
- **Nullability**: which fields may be missing, and under what conditions.
- **Latency**: how quickly records arrive after the real-world event (e.g., "95% of trades arrive within 2 seconds" or "fundamentals delivered by 06:00 T+1").
- **Uniqueness and keys**: what constitutes a unique record (e.g., instrument, date, provider).
- **Versioning and change policy**: how schema changes are announced and rolled out.

Why does this matter for LLMs? Because retrieval-augmented generation encourages direct, self-service use of data. When prompt templates, retrieval logic, or model-side tools implicitly assume that "this field is always present" or "this price is always end-of-day," they are relying on a contract. Making that contract explicit and machine-checked moves you from wishful thinking to engineering.

Data Quality Checks: Operationalizing the Contract

A contract without enforcement is just documentation. Data quality checks turn expectations into executable tests that run as part of the ingestion and transformation pipelines.

You can organize quality checks into four broad categories:

Completeness.
Are all expected records present?

- Check that you received data for all trading days up to yesterday.
- Verify that each instrument in your universe has at least one price per day.
- Confirm that fundamental datasets cover your full issuer universe within expected lags.

Validity.
Do field values fall within allowed ranges and domains?

- Prices and volumes should be non-negative and below plausible maximums.
- Enumerated fields (e.g., exchange code, currency) must match allowed values.
- Dates should lie within reasonable windows (no trades in year 1900).

Uniqueness and consistency.
Are key assumptions about duplicates and referential integrity satisfied?

- No two records with the same (instrument, date, source) combination, unless explicitly modeled as corrections.
- All foreign keys (e.g., instrument IDs in trades) must exist in the reference master.

Cross-source reconciliation.
Do different sources agree where they should?

- Compare closing prices from two vendors for the same instrument and day; flag large discrepancies.
- Reconcile portfolio-level P&L aggregates with individual trade and position records.

When checks fail, the pipeline should:

1. **Record the failure** with enough context (dataset, field, threshold, sample records).
2. **Decide an action**: reject the batch, quarantine suspicious records, or proceed with warnings depending on severity and downstream impact.
3. **Expose the status** to consumers. LLM applications, for example, may choose to ignore data marked "degraded quality" or adjust their explanations accordingly.

Over time, quality metrics themselves become valuable signals. A sudden spike in missing prices for a particular venue might indicate an upstream outage, not a market event. A well-instrumented ingestion system lets you distinguish the two.

Lineage: Making Every Number Traceable

Lineage answers two foundational questions:

1. **"Where did this data come from?"**

2. **"How was it transformed to reach its current form?"**

In finance, these are not philosophical questions; regulators, auditors, and risk managers often require precise answers, especially when models influence trading decisions.

There are two complementary levels of lineage:

Dataset-level lineage.
This describes dependencies between datasets or tables:

- "The daily_returns table is derived from prices_clean and corporate_actions."
- "The llm_vector_index for filings depends on the filings_parsed table and the issuer_master reference data."

Dataset-level lineage is often represented as a directed acyclic graph (DAG) in your orchestration tool. It is useful for impact analysis: if a vendor feed changes, which downstream products are affected?

Record- and field-level lineage.
For high-stakes use cases, you may need to know which specific records contributed to a value:

- A daily return might depend on two price records (close today, close yesterday) and one corporate action record (a split).
- A point-in-time leverage ratio might depend on a specific row from a particular 10-K filing version and an FX rate at the time.

Capturing such fine-grained lineage requires systematic tagging during transformations:

- Each record carries a **source identifier** (vendor, system) and **ingestion timestamp**.
- Transformations record which input records were combined to produce each output record, sometimes via surrogate keys or join logs.

- Versioning systems ensure that you can reproduce the exact transformation code and configuration used.

For LLM-based systems, lineage is the bridge between natural-language explanations and underlying facts. When an LLM says, "The company's debt-to-equity ratio increased from 1.3x to 1.8x between 2021 and 2022," it should be possible to:

- Retrieve the exact rows from the feature store that contain those ratios.
- Trace those ratios back to balance sheet line items in specific filed documents.
- Show which corporate actions or FX conversions were applied and when.

That is how "explainability" moves from a marketing slogan to something auditable.

Point-in-Time Stores: Defending Against Look-Ahead Bias

All of the above—ingestion, normalization, quality checks, lineage—come together in the design of *point-in-time stores*. These are data stores that answer queries as of a given historical moment *using only information that was available at that moment*.

Why is this crucial?

- **Backtesting integrity.** If your historical features use revised or restated data that was not known at the time, performance estimates will be inflated.
- **LLM credibility.** If an LLM analyzing a 2018 scenario accidentally uses a 2020 restatement, it will generate explanations that seem precise but are historically impossible.

A point-in-time store typically relies on:

Effective-time and load-time stamps.
Each record carries:

- An *effective time* (e.g., period end date, trade time).
- A *load or publication time* (when the information became known to your system).

A query for "features available on 2019-03-01 at 09:30 New York time" will select only records with load times less than or equal to that instant, even if later restatements exist.

Immutability of historical snapshots.
Once written, past snapshots should not be overwritten. If a restatement occurs, you add a new version with a later load time rather than rewriting history. This allows you to:

- Re-run backtests as they would have looked with the knowledge available at the time.
- Analyze the effect of restatements or methodology changes on strategy performance.

Integration with lineage.
Because load times and source identifiers are part of the record, you can answer questions like:

- "Which vendor's data did we rely on for this feature at that time?"
- "Was this feature based on a preliminary release or a restated filing?"

For LLM workflows, point-in-time stores act as the canonical retrieval source for structured features and sometimes even for document embeddings (e.g., using only filings and news available before a given date when simulating historical decision-making).

Bringing It All Together for LLM and Analytics Layers

From the perspective of an autonomous analyst built on transformers and retrieval-augmented generation, all of this data engineering can be summarized in a single promise:

> Whenever the model retrieves a fact or a feature, that item is timely, quality-checked, and traceable.

In practical terms, this means:

- Retrieval functions consult curated, point-in-time stores, not raw or ad-hoc tables.
- Prompt templates can refer to quality flags and lineage metadata, asking the model to qualify its answers when data is incomplete or conflicting.
- Debugging odd model behavior becomes feasible: you can trace a suspicious explanation back through the feature store to raw records and, if necessary, to vendor-level anomalies.

The next sections will build on this foundation, showing how to engineer features and vector knowledge graphs on top of these governed stores, and how to extend the same principles to streaming, real-time pipelines. But the core lesson remains: in retrieval-augmented finance, the reliability of your LLM is, in the end, the reliability of your ingestion, quality, and lineage pipelines.

4.2 Feature Engineering and Vectorized Knowledge Graphs

In the previous section we built the plumbing: ingestion pipelines, quality checks, and lineage that deliver clean, point-in-time data. We are now ready to turn that governed raw material into something models and LLMs can use directly.

This section has two closely linked goals:

- To show how to construct *financial features* from prices, fundamentals, and events in a way that is aligned across entities and time, and robust against leakage.
- To show how to represent the combined world of structured data and unstructured documents as a *vectorized knowledge graph*, so that retrieval-augmented LLMs can reason over both numbers and narrative with the same underlying map of the market.

Throughout, we will focus on practical intuitions: what each construct represents, how it is computed at a high level, and how it fits into an LLM-driven workflow.

From Clean Data to Model-Ready Features

Governed data by itself is not yet a trading signal. It is the equivalent of accounting ledgers: precise but not directly actionable. Feature engineering is the process of turning those ledgers and market observations into compact, informative descriptors of an entity's state at a given time.

What Counts as a Feature in Finance?

In a financial context, a *feature* is any quantity or categorical label that describes an instrument, issuer, portfolio, or macro entity at a defined time. Examples include:

- A stock's 20-day realized volatility.
- A company's net debt-to-EBITDA ratio based on its latest filing.
- A liquidity metric such as average daily dollar volume.
- A factor exposure (e.g., sensitivity to the value or momentum factor).
- An event flag such as "earnings announcement within the next 3 trading days."

Notice two aspects:

- **Entity specificity**: every feature is *about* something concrete (a security, an issuer, a sector, a macro index).
- **Time specificity**: every feature is *as of* a particular time, defined using the point-in-time machinery from the previous section.

If you cannot clearly answer "for whom?" and "as of when?" for a feature, that feature is not safe for backtesting or LLM use.

Core Feature Families

We briefly survey the main families of features you will typically engineer.

Return and volatility features.

From cleaned price series you can derive:

- *Simple or log returns* over different horizons (1-day, 5-day, 1-month).
- *Realized volatility*, often computed as the rolling standard deviation of daily (or intraday) returns over a fixed window.
- *Drawdown measures*, such as the percentage decline from a rolling maximum.

These capture how an instrument has behaved in the recent past-its momentum, risk, and downside experience.

Fundamental and leverage features.

From filings and fundamentals you can build ratios and trend indicators:

- Profitability metrics like gross margin or return on equity.
- Capital structure metrics such as leverage, interest coverage, and proportion of fixed vs. floating-rate debt.
- Growth indicators, for example year-over-year revenue growth or capex intensity.

Each such feature must be tied to the *filing date and acceptance time*, not just the period end, to avoid hindsight.

Liquidity and microstructure features.

From trades and quotes:

- Average daily volume and traded value.
- Bid-ask spreads, depth at best bid/ask, and order book imbalance.
- Turnover and share turnover relative to free float.

These features are particularly important in live deployment, where an LLM might be asked to reason about how realistic it is to execute suggested trades.

Event and calendar features.

From corporate actions, calendars, and news:

- Flags such as "post-earnings announcement" or "pre-dividend ex-date."
- Trading-day counters like "days since last earnings" or "days until known macro release."
- Binary markers of corporate events (e.g., M&A announcement, guidance change).

Event features act as anchors for both structured models and LLM prompts ("explain the move after the guidance cut").

Entity-Time Alignment: One Row per Entity per Moment

Once you have feature recipes, the next challenge is putting them into a consistent structure. A powerful mental model is:

> For each entity and each relevant time, we want one well-defined *feature vector* that uses only information available at that time.

Why Alignment Matters

Imagine two features:

- 20-day realized volatility, computed from daily close prices.
- Latest leverage ratio, computed from the most recent filing.

Suppose you want to train a model that uses both features on a common schedule, say daily at the close. If volatility is computed daily but leverage is updated only when new filings arrive, how do you align them?

The standard solution:

- For each trading day and instrument, compute volatility from past prices *up to that day*.
- For each trading day and issuer, carry forward the most recently filed leverage ratio whose publication time is earlier than or equal to that day's close.

The resulting daily "feature row" for a stock on a given date combines:

- A volatility measure that genuinely reflects the last 20 trading days.
- A leverage ratio that was truly known at that moment (no future filings).

This is *entity-time alignment*: every feature row matches a single entity (security or issuer) and a single "as-of" time, with each feature computed using only past or current information.

Practical Design of Feature Tables

In practice you will maintain one or more *feature tables* with the following characteristics:

- A primary key like (entity_id, as_of_time).
- Columns for each feature (returns, volatilities, ratios, event flags).

- Metadata columns such as data quality flags and feature versions.

These tables sit on top of your point-in-time store. Under the hood, calculating one row may require:

- Joining multiple base tables (prices, fundamentals, corporate actions).
- Applying rolling-window transformations.
- Respecting load times and publication times to avoid including future data.

For an LLM, these feature tables are the "numeric backbone" behind its narrative answers. When the model explains that "this stock has recently become riskier while leverage remains high," it is really summarizing a handful of structured features from such a table.

Avoiding Leakage: The Invisible Enemy in Feature Design

Leakage occurs when features or labels contain information that would not have been known at the decision time. It is invisible in-sample but devastating out-of-sample. LLMs, with their fluency and ability to connect scattered signals, can make leakage even more dangerous: they will confidently weave leaked information into plausible explanations.

Three common leakage traps are worth highlighting.

Using Restated Fundamentals as if They Were Original

Filings are often restated. If you build leverage or earnings features from the latest available data in your warehouse-without respecting load times-you silently inject future information into past periods.

The remedy is straightforward but non-negotiable:

- Store each version of a filing with its own *load or acceptance timestamp*.
- At a given as-of time, select only the latest version whose load time is not later than the as-of time.

This is where the point-in-time infrastructure from the previous section becomes directly relevant to feature engineering.

Look-Ahead Labels and Event Windows

Suppose you label days as "1" if the stock outperforms the market by more than 5% *in the next 20 days*, and "0" otherwise. That is acceptable, because the label is explicitly about the future. The leakage risk appears when you allow features to peek past the label definition point, for example:

- Computing "post-event" volatility using a window that includes returns after the decision time.
- Using the entire minute-level order book on the event day, even if your decision is supposed to happen at the open.

The safe pattern is to:

- Clearly define the decision time relative to each label.
- Restrict features to data no later than that decision time.

Survivorship and selection bias

If your universe of entities only includes those that survive to the present (for example, current index constituents), any feature computed on historical data will be biased. LLMs trained on such features may mistakenly explain "persistent quality" where in fact you have simply excluded past failures.

Defenses include:

- Maintaining historical membership lists (e.g., past index constituents).
- Including delisted or bankrupt entities in your feature tables.
- Tagging features with universe definitions so that LLM prompts can qualify the scope of any statement ("among current S&P 500 constituents...").

In short, leakage is not just a backtest issue; it is a credibility issue for any autonomous analyst that claims to be learning from history.

From Features to Vectorized Knowledge Graphs

So far we have focused on structured features: numeric and categorical descriptors of entities. But markets are also driven by text: filings, earnings call transcripts, research notes, news, social media, and more. LLMs shine on this unstructured side. The crucial design question is: *how do we connect the world of vectors (text embeddings) with the world of structured features and entities?*

The answer in this book is the *vectorized knowledge graph.*

What Is a Vectorized Knowledge Graph?

A traditional knowledge graph represents entities and their relationships as nodes and edges:

- Nodes: issuers, securities, sectors, indices, macro indicators, documents.
- Edges: "issuer–owns–security," "security–belongs to–sector," "filing–about–issuer," "news–mentions–security."

A vectorized knowledge graph adds:

- **Dense vector embeddings** attached to text-bearing nodes (filings, news, transcripts, research notes), representing their semantic content.
- **Timestamps and entity IDs** attached to nodes and edges, tying each piece of text to the same entity-time axis used in your feature tables.

In effect, the graph becomes the central "map" of your market world, and embeddings are annotations that make it searchable and comparable via similarity.

At this point it is helpful to visualize the structure we are aiming for.

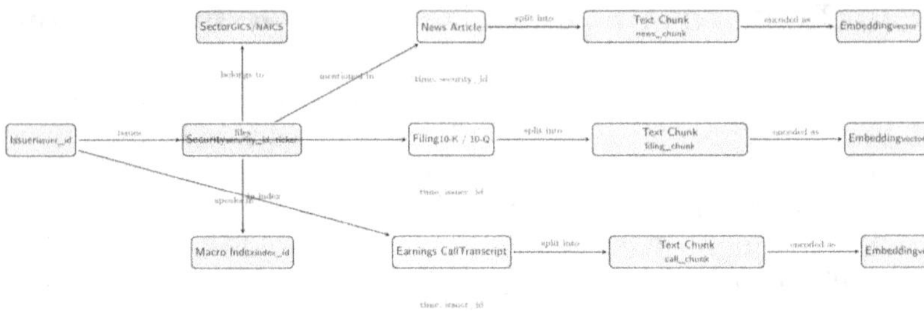

This conceptual diagram illustrates the core idea: entities such as issuers and securities are connected to documents; documents are broken into chunks; chunks are embedded into vectors. Every node and many edges carry both IDs and timestamps, creating an integrated space where LLMs can retrieve text and numbers about the same thing at the same time.

Anchoring Text to Entities and Time

A key design principle of the vectorized knowledge graph is:

> Every document fragment must be explicitly anchored to one or more entities and a time interval.

Without this, you cannot reliably combine text with structured features.

Entity Linking

Entity linking is the process of connecting a piece of text to the entities it refers to. For financial text, this often involves:

- Recognizing tickers, company names, and instrument identifiers in text.
- Resolving ambiguities (e.g., "Apple" the company vs. the fruit; "GM" the ticker vs. other acronyms).
- Attaching a canonical entity ID from your master data (issuer_id, security_id).

For a 10-K filing, entity linking is usually straightforward: the document's issuer is known. For news articles or research notes, it can be more challenging; an article may mention multiple companies, sectors, and macro indicators. In the graph:

- The document node (or even individual chunks) may have edges to several entities.
- Each edge can include metadata like "primary subject" vs. "secondary mention."

This matters for retrieval. When an LLM asks, "What recent news might explain the jump in volatility for this stock?", your retrieval layer should prioritize news chunks primarily about that security.

Time Anchoring

Text is inherently fuzzy in time. A news article might report on an event that happened last week and was published today; an earnings call transcript discusses the past quarter and future guidance. For retrieval-augmented finance, we at least need:

- A *publication or ingestion time*: when the document became available to the market (or to your system).
- Optionally, event-specific times for major facts mentioned in the text (e.g., merger announcement date).

When we attach publication time and entity IDs to document nodes and chunk nodes, we can:

- Restrict retrieval to documents that were available as of a given backtest time.
- Time-align retrieved text with structured features (volatility, leverage, liquidity) computed at the same as-of time.

This time anchoring is how we prevent an LLM from "reading tomorrow's newspaper" in historical simulations.

Embedding Documents and Chunks

Once documents are linked to entities and time, the next step is to make them searchable via similarity. This is where embeddings come in.

Why Chunking Matters

Most embedding models operate on text segments of bounded length. Filings, transcripts, and long news stories must be split into smaller *chunks*. Chunking should respect both:

- **Semantic coherence**: avoid splitting sentences or tightly connected paragraphs.
- **Contextual retrieval**: keep related information together so that a retrieved chunk is self-contained enough for the LLM to use.

Each chunk then becomes a node in the knowledge graph, with attributes such as:

- Parent document ID (so we can reconstruct full context if needed).
- Entity IDs inherited from or refined relative to the parent.
- Publication time (and possibly other event times).
- The embedding vector produced by an encoder model.

Storing and Indexing Vectors

Embeddings for chunks are stored in a vector index that supports similarity search (e.g., nearest neighbors under cosine or dot-product similarity). Conceptually, you can think of the index as an additional "view" on the knowledge graph:

- Each entry corresponds to a chunk node.
- The entry stores the embedding and a pointer back to the graph node and its attributes (entity IDs, times, document type).

When an LLM or application issues a semantic search query such as "supply chain disruptions impacting semiconductor manufacturers," the system:

- Encodes the query into an embedding.
- Searches the vector index for similar chunk vectors.
- Filters candidates using graph metadata (e.g., only filings or only chunks linked to a given issuer universe and time range).
- Returns the text of the top chunks, plus their structured context, to the LLM.

This is how the unstructured side of the market becomes navigable with the same rigor as structured features.

Hybrid Retrieval: Combining Graph, Features, and Vectors

The full power of the vectorized knowledge graph appears when we combine three ingredients:

- The **graph structure**, describing relationships between entities and documents.
- The **feature tables**, providing numeric and categorical descriptors of entities at specific times.
- The **vector index**, enabling semantic search over text chunks.

Consider an example workflow:

> "Explain the main drivers behind the recent increase in volatility for stock X, using both numbers and recent company communications."

A retrieval-augmented system might proceed as follows:

- Use the graph to find the security node for X and its issuer node.
- Look up recent feature rows for X: realized volatility, returns, liquidity, event flags.
- Identify a period where volatility increased significantly.
- Using graph edges and time constraints, search for filings, earnings calls, and news associated with the issuer during that period.
- Use the vector index to retrieve chunks of text within those documents most semantically related to risk, guidance changes, or surprises.
- Package both the structured feature snapshots and retrieved text chunks into the LLM prompt, with clear indications of dates and entities.

The LLM's answer then reflects not just surface-level pattern matching, but a deep integration of:

- Quantitative signals (volatility, drawdowns, leverage changes).
- Qualitative context (management commentary, reported issues, external news).
- The structural relationships between them (issuer-security-sector).

Because everything is anchored to the same entity-time axis, the explanation is historically consistent and auditable.

Design Principles for LLM-Friendly Feature and Graph Layers

To close this section, it is useful to summarize a few design principles that keep feature engineering and vectorized knowledge graphs aligned with the needs of retrieval-augmented LLM systems:

- **Always think in entity-time coordinates.** Any feature, document, or chunk that cannot be clearly tied to an entity and a time is a liability for backtesting and retrieval.
- **Treat leakage as a first-class risk.** Leverage your point-in-time store and lineage metadata in every feature computation and document retrieval, especially in historical simulations.
- **Use the graph as the organizing backbone.** Let entities and relationships in the knowledge graph define how features and documents hang together; avoid ad-hoc, one-off tables that bypass the graph.
- **Expose metadata to the LLM.** Quality flags, event types, and versions can be surfaced in prompts, allowing the model to qualify its answers ("data for this period is incomplete").
- **Keep chunks and features small but meaningful.** Overly large chunks confuse retrieval; overly narrow features make prompts unwieldy. Design both with the LLM's token and attention limits in mind.

In the next section we will extend these ideas into the streaming, real-time world: updating features and graph edges intraday, incrementally refreshing vector indexes, and ensuring that even ultra-low-latency insights remain traceable back through the same disciplined data backbone.

4.3 Streaming and Real-Time Data Infrastructure

In the first section of this chapter we built reliable batch pipelines: data flows from raw feeds into governed, point-in-time stores with explicit contracts, quality checks, and lineage. In the second section we used those stores to engineer aligned features and to construct vectorized knowledge graphs that bridge structured and unstructured data.

We now turn to the setting where time pressures are tighter: intraday trading, real-time risk, and LLM tools that respond to events as they happen. The goal is to extend the same principles—contracts, validation, traceability—into *streaming architectures* that support:

- Intraday analytics and monitoring.
- Event-driven triggers (for example, "run this analysis when a stock gaps more than 5% after earnings").
- Low-latency retrieval for LLM-powered tools (for example, a chatbot that can explain the last hour's price moves using fresh news and order book signals).

We will build up the ideas gradually, starting from what makes real-time financial data special, then introducing key streaming concepts, and finally showing how to wire them into retrieval-augmented LLM workflows.

What Changes in the Real-Time Setting?

Conceptually, batch and streaming systems solve the same problem: transform raw data into useful, trustworthy information. The difference is *when* you do the work and how much delay you can tolerate.

In a batch world:

- Data for a trading day might arrive as a single file at night.
- You process everything at once, perhaps with a few hours of slack.
- Users interact with yesterday's data or curated historical views.

In a streaming world:

- Data arrives continuously as events: ticks, order book updates, new trades, news headlines, chat messages, internal orders.
- You process events as they come, maintaining rolling aggregates and state.
- Users want answers based on data that may be only seconds or milliseconds old.

This shift has several implications for our previously established themes.

Data contracts now include latency. In batch pipelines, a contract might say "the vendor delivers yesterday's prices by 06:00." In streaming, contracts must specify:

- Typical and worst-case delays between the real-world event and its appearance in your stream.
- Acceptable rates of out-of-order or late events.

Quality checks must be incremental and non-blocking. You cannot stop the stream for hours when you detect an anomaly. Instead you must:

- Detect schema changes and value anomalies quickly.
- Decide whether to drop, quarantine, or pass through suspicious events with downgraded quality flags.

Lineage must support replay. In batch mode, rerunning a job is straightforward. In streaming mode, you must log every event and every transformation statefully so that you can:

- Reconstruct historical state at any time.
- Recompute features (and model outputs) as if you were "replaying" the market.

With these differences in mind, we next introduce the basic building blocks of a streaming system.

Streams, Events, and Stateful Operators

At the heart of a streaming architecture is the idea of an *event stream*. Instead of files or tables, you deal with sequences of records that arrive over time. For example:

- A trades stream: each event is a single executed trade on an exchange (instrument, price, size, timestamp, venue).
- An order_book stream: each event is an update to the bid-ask ladder.
- A news stream: each event is a new headline or article metadata record.
- An internal orders stream: each event is a new order or state transition in your own trading system.

Events flow through a network of *operators*:

- **Stateless operators** transform each event independently: schema mapping, field renaming, type casting, simple filtering.
- **Stateful operators** keep memory of past events: rolling averages, VWAP, inventory levels, alert conditions.

These operators are typically orchestrated on top of a message bus or log (such as Kafka-like systems) or a dedicated stream processing framework. The implementation details vary, but the conceptual pattern stays stable.

Event Time vs. Processing Time

One concept that often confuses beginners is the difference between *event time* and *processing time*:

- **Event time** is when the event actually occurred in the real world (for example, the exchange's trade timestamp).
- **Processing time** is when your system processed that event.

In an ideal world, these two would be almost identical. In reality, networks jitter, feeds go down, and systems restart. Events can arrive late or out-of-order.

This matters because many financial quantities are defined in event time:

- A 5-minute VWAP from 10:00:00 to 10:04:59 should only include trades whose *event time* falls in that window, even if some arrive late.
- Intraday P&L at 11:00 should reflect all trades and prices that have event time up to 11:00, regardless of when they were processed.

Proper streaming systems therefore make event time a first-class field and structure their computations around it. Processing time still matters—for latency and resource management—but event time defines the "truth" of the market.

Windows, Watermarks, and Late Data

To compute intraday features such as rolling volatility or VWAP, we need to group events into finite windows of event time. Streaming frameworks typically offer windowing constructs:

- **Tumbling windows**: non-overlapping fixed-length intervals (for example, every 1 minute).
- **Sliding windows**: overlapping windows (for example, last 15 minutes, updated every minute).
- **Session windows**: intervals delimited by periods of inactivity.

The main challenge is dealing with late events. How long should the system wait for more data before declaring a window "final"? The usual tool here is the *watermark*.

A **watermark** is an estimate of the maximum event time that the system has seen "up to now." Any events with event time older than "watermark minus tolerance" are treated as too late and may be dropped or handled specially.

For instance:

- The system maintains a watermark that lags behind the maximum observed event time by, say, 2 seconds.

- When the watermark passes the end of a 1-second VWAP window, that window's result is emitted.
- If an event belonging to that window arrives later, the system can either ignore it or, in more advanced setups, emit a correction.

For high-frequency trading, the tolerance is very small. For news feeds or alternative data, you may accept larger lags.

Quality and lineage considerations appear again:

- Windows should be tagged with completeness flags: "final," "provisional," "corrected."
- If corrections are issued, the lineage system should track both original and corrected values.

These annotations are critical if you later train models or query LLMs based on historical streaming aggregates.

Exactly-Once Semantics and Idempotence

In batch mode, duplicates and partial failures are usually obvious. In streaming, where systems retry operations and reprocess logs, it is easy to double-count events or miss some entirely.

Two related concepts address this:

Exactly-once semantics. A streaming pipeline has exactly-once semantics if each input event affects the downstream state (and outputs) as if it had been processed *once and only once*, even if the underlying infrastructure does retries or restarts.

Achieving true exactly-once behavior is technically complex, but modern frameworks approximate it using:

- Idempotent writes (writing the same update twice has the same effect as writing it once).
- Transactional checkpoints of operator state aligned with message offsets in the log.

Idempotence and keys. From a data-engineering perspective, you can help by designing schemas and keys that support idempotence:

- Ensure that each event has a stable identifier (for example, trade ID).
- Design aggregations so that emitting the same aggregate twice with the same key overwrites or merges cleanly, rather than doubling counts.

For an LLM-powered system, exactly-once semantics and idempotence translate into consistency: a user asking about "trades in the last minute" should not see counts or VWAPs that sporadically spike due to duplicate processing.

Streaming Feature Computation

With these building blocks—event time, windows, watermarks, and exactly-once semantics—we can now compute intraday features in a streaming fashion.

Examples include:

- **Intraday VWAP** per instrument over sliding windows (for example, last 5 minutes).
- **Rolling realized volatility** from intraday returns.
- **Microstructure indicators**: order book imbalance, spread changes, trade direction imbalance.
- **Real-time position and inventory risk**: net position by instrument, sector, or desk; unrealized P&L; margin utilization.

Compared to batch features:

- The computations are expressed as continuous aggregations over streams, rather than as SQL over static tables.

- They must be designed to cope gracefully with late or missing data, producing provisional results that may later be corrected.
- They run constantly, maintaining state in memory or in distributed stores.

Despite these differences, we should maintain continuity with the batch world:

- Streaming feature definitions should be as close as possible to their end-of-day counterparts, to ease interpretation.
- The outputs of streaming pipelines should be periodically checkpointed into the same or compatible feature stores used by batch systems.
- Quality flags and lineage metadata should be captured at each step, just as in batch pipelines.

Streaming into Vector Stores and Knowledge Graphs

Real-time is not only about numbers. For an autonomous analyst, the flow of text is equally important: news headlines, short bulletins, streaming social messages, and intraday regulatory announcements.

To bring these into the vectorized knowledge graph introduced earlier, we extend the streaming architecture as follows:

- A `news` or `text_events` stream carries new documents or updates (for example, "headline at 10:03: market reacts to guidance cut").
- A stateless operator performs light cleaning and attaches basic metadata (source, feed, raw timestamps).
- An entity-linking operator identifies which issuers, securities, sectors, or indices the text refers to, and attaches IDs.
- A chunking and embedding operator splits longer text into chunks and passes each through an embedding model to produce vectors.

- The resulting chunk nodes and embeddings are written:
- As edges/nodes into the knowledge graph store (for structural relationships).
- Into a vector index that is updated incrementally.

Two important design choices arise here:

Update frequency and latency. You must decide how quickly new text becomes visible in retrieval:

- For ultra-low-latency strategies (for example, reacting to breaking news within seconds), you may accept approximate or partial embeddings produced by a fast, lightweight model.
- For human-facing research tools, a delay of tens of seconds or minutes may be acceptable, allowing more accurate or expensive embedding models.

Consistency with batch embeddings. If you have a large historical corpus embedded with one model, but real-time streams use a different (perhaps more recent) model, you must:

- Record which embedding model and version was used for each chunk (as metadata).
- Consider periodic re-embedding for important subsets to maintain comparability.

Again, lineage is the glue: any retrieved text chunk should carry along its embedding model version, entity links, and ingestion time, so that LLM prompts can reason about freshness and reliability.

Event-Driven Triggers for LLM Workflows

One of the main benefits of combining streaming infrastructure with LLMs is the ability to respond to specific events with rich analysis, not just numeric alerts.

Consider a few patterns:

Price-move triggers. A stateful streaming operator monitors intraday returns and volatility. When a threshold is crossed (for example, "stock X down more than 5% on the day, with volume $> 2\times$ average"), it emits an analysis_request event. Downstream:

- A retrieval service uses the knowledge graph and vector index to pull recent news, filings, and call transcripts related to X.
- A feature service extracts current intraday and recent historical features for X and its peers.
- An LLM is invoked with a prompt template that includes these materials, asking it to "summarize plausible drivers of today's move, and compare to similar historical episodes."

News triggers. Alternatively, a high-impact news classifier runs on the news stream. When a headline is classified as "earnings surprise" or "guidance cut" for a covered name, it triggers:

- Real-time feature recomputation for the affected instruments and sectors.
- An LLM-based "impact note" that contextualizes the news using historical reactions, current positioning, and factor exposures.

Risk and limit triggers. Streaming risk calculations track intraday P&L and exposure. When thresholds are breached, an event triggers an LLM to generate a plain-language explanation tailored to human risk managers ("top 5 contributors to today's drawdown," "largest concentrated bets relative to limits").

Technically, all of these workflows are variants of a single pattern:

- A streaming operator computes conditions and emits events when they are met.
- A retrieval and feature layer, built on the same batch/streaming backbone, assembles relevant data.

- An LLM is invoked with structured prompts that reference that data.

The key is that the event-driven side (triggers) and the analytical side (retrieval + LLM) share the same data contracts, quality checks, and lineage.

Dual Paths: Ultra-Low-Latency vs. Explainable Analysis

In practice, many trading organizations separate their real-time logic into two paths:

- An **ultra-low-latency path** that makes or supports execution decisions at sub-second to millisecond timescales.
- A **slower, explainable analysis path** that operates at human-relevant timescales (seconds to minutes), ideal for LLM-based tooling.

The ultra-low-latency path:

- Is often implemented as close as possible to the exchange or execution engine.
- Uses highly optimized, specialized code with minimal dependencies.
- Relies on a narrow set of hand-crafted, robust signals.

The explainable path:

- Reuses the same underlying data streams (or copies thereof), but allows more complex transformations and richer context.
- Writes its outputs—features, embeddings, intermediate aggregations—into stores accessible to LLM services and analysts.

- Emphasizes lineage and audibility, so that human users can trust the explanations.

Designing your streaming architecture with both paths in mind leads to several good practices:

- Use shared schemas and contracts for core streams, so both paths interpret events identically.
- Ensure that even the ultra-low-latency decisions are logged in a way that the explainable path can reconstruct ("why did we act at this moment?").
- Allow LLM tools to cross-reference real-time decisions with batch and historical context, grounded in the same knowledge graph.

Auditable Real-Time Systems

The central message of this chapter has been that retrieval-augmented finance is only as sound as its data engineering. In the real-time setting, that message becomes more urgent, not less.

An *auditable* real-time system can answer questions like:

- "Which exact ticks and news items did we see before making this decision?"
- "What were the intermediate feature values, and how were they computed?"
- "If we replay the event stream with today's improved code, how does the output change?"

To support such questions, your streaming infrastructure should:

- Persist raw event logs for sufficient periods, with stable offsets and IDs.

- Periodically checkpoint operator state and emitted aggregates into stores that share the batch world's lineage framework.
- Tag all outputs with metadata: source streams, processing timestamps, software versions, quality flags.

When an LLM-based analyst explains an intraday episode, it relies on this machinery: the features it cites, the documents it quotes, and the triggers it responds to are all products of a streaming system designed not just for speed, but for transparency.

In summary, streaming and real-time infrastructure extends the batch foundations of ingestion, quality, and lineage into the time-critical domain. Doing so lets you build LLM-powered tools that are both responsive and trustworthy—helping human and automated traders navigate not only what happened, but what is happening *right now*, with the same level of rigor that regulators and risk managers demand from end-of-day reports.

Chapter 5

LLM System Design and Agentic Workflows

Markets move faster than any human research process, yet most LLM setups still treat the model as a chatty assistant rather than a disciplined, tool-using analyst. In this chapter we design systems-not prompts in isolation-that combine structured instructions, retrieval, function calling, and agentic workflows into repeatable pipelines. You will learn how to turn a raw model into a controllable market analyst that can fetch data, justify its answers, and coordinate multistep investigations with minimal human supervision.

5.1 Prompt Engineering and Function Calling

In the previous chapter we treated large language models (LLMs) as *reasoning engines*: systems that can read text, recognize patterns, and explain market behavior. In this section we take the next step and treat the model as a *controller*—a deterministic front-end for your data and trading tools. Instead of "chatting" with the model and hoping for a useful answer, you will design prompts and tool interfaces so that, given the same inputs, the system reliably produces the same structured outputs and the same tool calls.

The central idea is simple but powerful: you want the LLM to behave less like an improvising macro strategist on a whiteboard and more like a junior analyst following a checklist and a set of dashboards. Prompt engineering shapes *what* the analyst tries to do and *how* it communicates. Function calling defines *which* external tools the analyst can use and *how* it asks for them. Together, they turn the model from a free-form text generator into an orchestrator of deterministic computations.

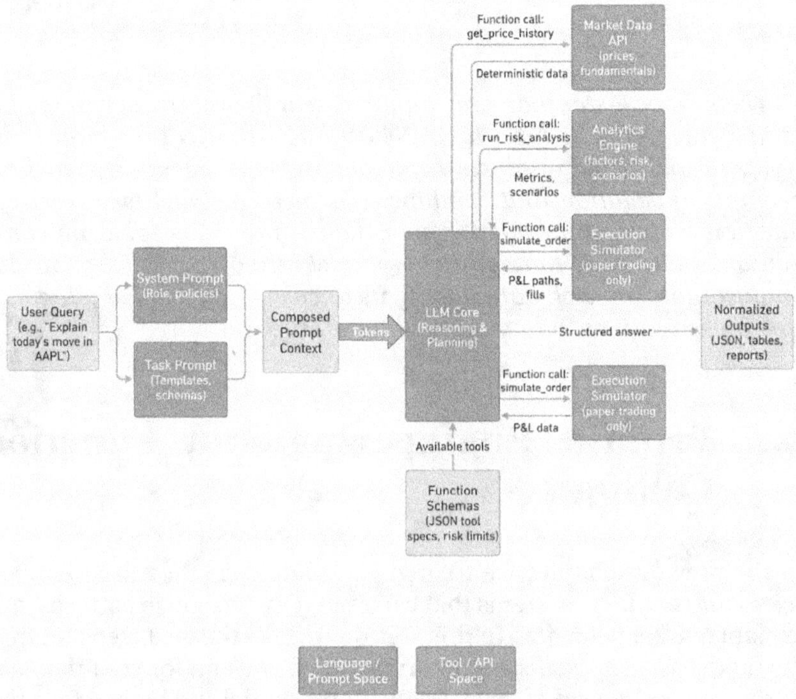

From "Chatty" Models to Controlled Analysts

Most users' first experience with an LLM is conversational. You ask: "What do you think about tech stocks?" and receive a fluent paragraph. For exploratory thinking, this can be useful, but in a trading or investment workflow, it is dangerous:

- The model may rely on stale training data instead of current market prices.
- It may improvise numbers, references, or even orders that do not exist.
- The same question asked twice may yield different, incompatible answers.

A production-grade "autonomous analyst" must behave differently. When you ask: "Summarize the last two quarters of AAPL earnings and flag changes in guidance," you want:

1. A repeatable sequence of steps: identify the ticker, locate the relevant transcripts, extract the right passages, compute simple diffs or metrics, then summarize.
2. A clear separation between *facts* (pulled from deterministic tools: data APIs, document search, analytics engines) and *narrative* (the LLM's synthesis of those facts).
3. Outputs in formats your downstream systems can consume: JSON fields, tagged tables, or fixed report templates, not arbitrary prose.

Prompt engineering provides the "operating manual" the model follows. Function calling gives it access to the calculators, databases, and simulators that guarantee numerical and operational correctness. We will start with prompt patterns and progress to tool interfaces, always with the goal of making the system predictable and auditable.

Core Prompting Patterns for Financial Tasks

At a high level, a prompt is just all the text you send to the model: instructions, examples, and context. For trading and investing, you should think of prompts as standardized forms, similar to templates for investment memos or risk reports.

We will focus on three elements:

1. Role and objective specification.
2. Input normalization.
3. Output normalization.

Role and Objective Specification

The system prompt is where you define *who* the model is supposed to be and *what* it is trying to optimize. For example:

- "You are a cautious macro analyst supporting a global multi-asset portfolio. You must never assume access to future data."
- "You are an equity research assistant focused on U.S. large-cap stocks. Your job is to transform raw data into standardized analytical outputs, not to recommend trades."

Specificity matters. Roles should include:

- **Domain**: macro, equity, credit, volatility, etc.
- **Risk posture**: cautious, exploratory, adversarial (for red-teaming assumptions).
- **Forbidden actions**: no live order placement, no guessing of missing numeric data, no use of proprietary information unless explicitly provided.

The objective reinforces *how* the model should trade off detail, speed, and conservatism. For a risk reviewer, you might say: "Err on the side of flagging too many potential risks, even if some are unlikely."

Input Normalization: Speak a Consistent Language

Humans adapt naturally to messy input. Models are more brittle. For consistent behavior, you should normalize how you present market questions:

- Use a fixed header with key fields: TASK, TICKER, UNIVERSE, DATE_AS_OF, HORIZON, CONSTRAINTS.
- Express dates in a standard format and always specify "as-of" dates when discussing historical scenarios.
- Decompose complex requests into sub-questions with labels, e.g., "(a) describe drivers of the move, (b) link to macro data, (c) highlight risks."

This "input normalization" makes it much easier for the model to map your prompts to the same downstream tools and output structures. It also makes your logs more analyzable: every query can be parsed by scripts.

Output Normalization: Schemas and Checklists

Free-form text is difficult to verify, compare, or feed into other systems. For a production analyst, you want the majority of outputs to follow a simple, repeating structure.

Two practical tools:

Schemas. Define explicit field names and expected types. For instance, when summarizing earnings:

- ticker: string
- fiscal_quarter: string (e.g., "Q2 2025")
- revenue_surprise_bps: integer
- eps_surprise_bps: integer
- guidance_change: enum (UP, DOWN, UNCH, N/A)
- key_drivers: list of short bullet strings

You instruct the model to *only* answer using this schema, typically in JSON form. Even if the model's internal reasoning is complex, the output is machine-usable.

Checklists. For narrative sections, define ordered lists of questions the model must answer. For example, a macro narrative template might require:

1. Which assets moved, by how much?
2. What immediate catalysts were visible at the time?
3. How do the moves relate to recent macro data or policy signals?
4. What alternative explanations should be considered?

By referencing these checklists in your prompts, you reduce omissions and make cross-comparison across days or assets more meaningful.

Zero-Shot, Few-Shot, and Chain-of-Thought in Practice

Within this framework, you can still choose among common prompting styles, but now they serve specific, engineering goals.

Zero-Shot Prompting

Zero-shot means you give the model only instructions and context, no examples. For instance:

> "Using the schema below, summarize the last two quarters of earnings for TICKER = AAPL as of DATE_AS_OF = 2025-06-30. Use only the information in the provided transcripts and tool outputs. Do not guess missing values."

With well-designed schemas and strong system prompts, zero-shot is often enough, especially once the model is connected to deterministic tools.

Few-Shot Prompting

Few-shot adds a small number of worked examples. This is especially helpful when:

- You want a distinctive "house style" for narratives.
- The schema is subtle (e.g., rating sentiment as "mildly positive" vs "strongly positive").
- You need the model to perform multi-step reasoning that is not obvious from the instruction alone.

In financial workflows, a few carefully chosen example memos or risk summaries can significantly stabilize output formatting and tone.

Chain-of-Thought Prompting

Chain-of-thought (CoT) instructs the model to "show its work" step by step before giving a final answer. For investment workflows, this is valuable but must be used thoughtfully:

- For complex attributions ("Explain the move in EURUSD over the last month using macro data and central bank communications"), CoT improves transparency and often quality.
- For time-sensitive tasks or simple extractions, CoT may add latency and verbosity without much benefit.

A practical compromise is to request CoT reasoning in a hidden internal section (for debugging or audit) while asking for a concise structured summary as the primary output.

From Prompts to Function Calls: The Bridge to Tools

So far we have focused on text: instructions, templates, schemas. To turn the model into a deterministic controller, we must now connect it to external tools—your market data, analytics, and simulation engines.

Function calling is the mechanism that allows the LLM to say, in effect: "To answer this, I need to call `get_price_history` with these parameters," and then incorporate the returned data into its reasoning. The model produces a structured object (typically JSON) describing the function and its arguments; your system executes that function, returns the result, and the model continues.

You can think of this as giving the model a calculator and data terminal. Instead of hallucinating numbers, it must ask your tools for them.

Designing Clear, Safe Function Schemas

A function schema defines:

- The function name (e.g., get_price_history).
- Each parameter's name, type, allowed values, and description.
- Any constraints or risk limits (e.g., maximum lookback window).

For example, a price history function might include:

- ticker: string, required, must be in your coverage universe.
- start_date, end_date: ISO dates, required; must satisfy start_date <= end_date.
- fields: enum list (e.g., ["close", "volume"]); no arbitrary field names.
- max_window_days: documented in the description; the model should be instructed not to exceed this.

The goal is to minimize ambiguity. If the LLM tries to call get_price_history with an invalid field, your validation layer should reject and optionally trigger a repair prompt ("The field 'mid' is not supported; please choose from ...").

You should embed risk and governance constraints directly into these schemas:

- Only paper-trading execution simulators are exposed; no live execution functions are visible to the model.
- Backtest functions enforce no-lookahead via their own parameters (e.g., as_of_date) and internal checks.
- Data-fetching functions cap the amount of data that can be pulled in one call, protecting cost and latency budgets.

Teaching the Model When to Use Which Tool

The function descriptions are your opportunity to guide tool selection. For each function, include:

- A concise description: "Use this to retrieve historical OHLCV for a single equity ticker."
- Clear "when to use" hints: "Call this when the user asks about price, returns, or volatility over time."
- Explicit "when not to use" hints: "Do not use for intraday tick data; instead call get_intraday_bars."

Your system prompt can reinforce this:

> "When you need factual market data, always use the available tools instead of relying on your internal knowledge. Prefer the get_fundamentals function for fundamentals, the get_price_history function for historical prices, and the run_risk_analysis function for risk metrics."

By combining function descriptions with core instructions, you push the model toward consistent tool usage patterns, which are easier to monitor and debug.

Reliability Strategies: Idempotence, Validation, and Policies

Even with good prompts and tool schemas, you still need mechanisms that turn your analyst into a reliable subsystem rather than an unpredictable black box. Three practical strategies are especially useful.

Enforcing Idempotent Behavior

Idempotence means: given the same prompt and the same available tools, the system should behave the same way. You can encourage this by:

- Using deterministic temperature settings (e.g., low or zero temperature in production flows).

- Making prompts explicit about sequence: "Always follow the steps: (1) restate the task, (2) decide which tools are needed, (3) call tools, (4) synthesize a structured answer."
- Logging and comparing function call traces for identical or similar prompts; large variations can indicate prompt drift or misunderstandings.

An idempotent analyst is easier to test: you can replay historical prompts and verify that the sequence of tool calls and outputs remains stable when your data and tools are unchanged.

Validation Layers for Tool Calls and Outputs

Never trust the model's function calls or outputs blindly. Simple validation layers can catch many issues:

Tool call validation. Before executing a function:

- Check all required parameters are present and correctly typed.
- Enforce range limits (e.g., no date window beyond 5 years).
- Confirm the requested ticker or instrument is in your allowed universe.

If validation fails, you can:

- Return an error to the model with a short description and let it repair the call.
- Abort the workflow and notify a human operator for critical flows.

Output validation. For structured outputs:

- Ensure JSON parses and all required fields are present.
- Run simple consistency checks (e.g., EPS surprise should equal reported minus consensus, within tolerance).
- Compare narrative claims against retrieved data where possible (e.g., if narrative says "revenue grew 10%", but data shows 3%, you can flag a discrepancy).

These checks do not need to be complex; even basic rules dramatically improve reliability.

Using Policies to Bound Behavior

Finally, embed explicit policies into both prompts and tools:

- **Scope policies**: "You only analyze instruments from the specified universe; if asked about others, explain that they are out of scope."
- **Data policies**: "Do not infer or fabricate proprietary data; if it is not provided via tools or context, state that it is unavailable."
- **Action policies**: "You may propose hypothetical trades, but you must not attempt to submit or modify live orders."

These policies should be repeated in the system prompt, referenced in function descriptions, and—where possible—enforced at the infrastructure level (for example, by not exposing any order-placement APIs to the model at all).

From Single Prompts to a Reusable Control Surface

As your autonomous analyst matures, your goal is to move from one-off prompts to a small library of reusable templates and function definitions that together act as a "control surface" for the system.

In practice, this means:

- A base system prompt defining global behavior and policies.
- A set of task prompts for common workflows: earnings summarization, macro event explanation, risk scenario analysis, corporate action digestion, and so on.
- A stable catalog of tools (functions) with well-documented schemas and constraints.
- Validation and logging around every tool call and structured output.

When a new requirement appears—say, "flag unusual options activity around major earnings events"—you should not start from scratch. Instead, you:

1. Identify which existing tools can supply the needed data (options chain, historical volume, event calendar).
2. Draft a new task prompt that composes these tools and reuses existing schemas for outputs (e.g., an "unusual activity" schema).
3. Add limited, well-motivated new tools only if necessary, with the same design discipline.

By designing prompts and function interfaces this way, you gradually evolve from an experimental chatbot into a structured, policy-bound, and auditable autonomous analyst—one that you can trust to sit alongside your other production trading systems.

5.2 Retrieval-Augmented Generation and Temporal Retrieval

In the previous section we made the LLM behave less like a chatty assistant and more like a controlled analyst by using prompt engineering and function calling. We treated the model as a *planner and controller* that decides which tools to use and how to structure its outputs. In this section we address a different but equally important issue: *where the information comes from.*

Out of the box, an LLM's knowledge is frozen at the time it was trained. It has a rough memory of past crises, famous companies, and macro relationships, but it does not "know" last quarter's earnings, yesterday's FOMC statement, or this morning's price action unless you provide that information at runtime. For an autonomous analyst, this is unacceptable. If you ask, "How did the market react to the 2024-2025 rate-cut cycle?" you do not want an answer based only on what was typical in past cycles; you want an answer grounded in actual data and documents from that period.

Retrieval-Augmented Generation (RAG) is the main pattern we use to solve this problem. Instead of letting the model guess from its frozen training set, we build a pipeline that:

- Stores relevant financial information (documents, transcripts, research notes, logs) in a searchable index.

- Retrieves the most relevant, time-appropriate pieces of information for a given question.

- Feeds those pieces into the model so that its answer is grounded in up-to-date and causally valid evidence.

Crucially, for markets we must make retrieval *temporal*: the analyst should only see information that would have been available as of a given decision time, and it should favor recent, high-quality sources over old, generic commentary. Otherwise, any backtest or historical scenario analysis risks "peeking into the future."

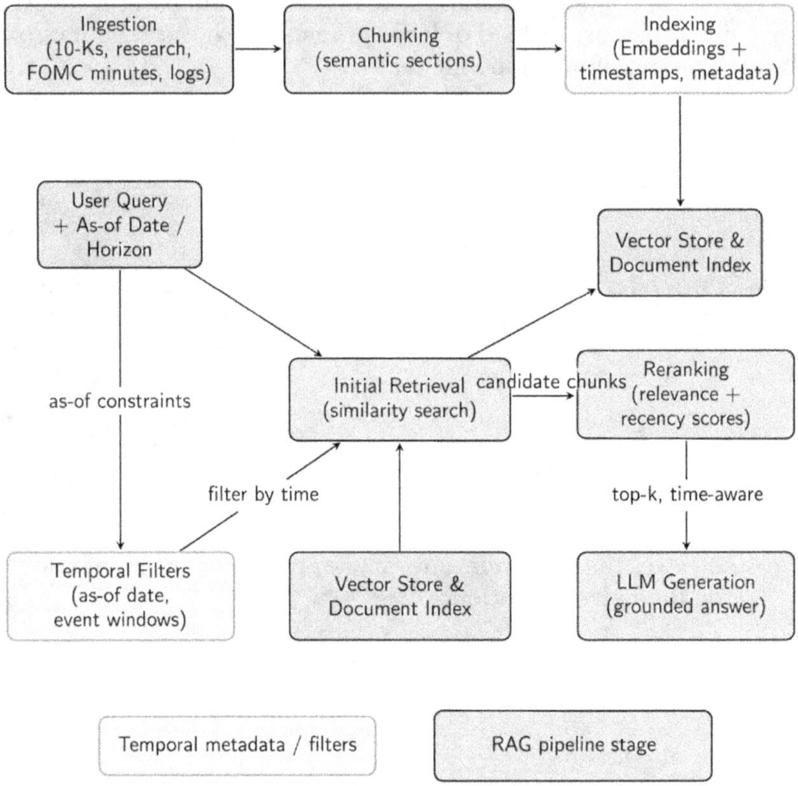

Why Retrieval Matters in Markets

To see why retrieval is not just convenient but essential, consider three typical questions:

- "Summarize the main risks highlighted in JPM's last three 10-K filings."
- "How did markets react to the September 2024 FOMC meeting?"
- "If we were deciding on this trade as of March 31, 2022, what information about this company would have been available?"

No matter how powerful the base model is, it:

- Cannot reliably reproduce the exact wording of 10-K risk factors without seeing the actual documents.
- Cannot "remember" the detailed intraday reaction to a specific FOMC meeting.
- Cannot automatically enforce the rule "only use information known as of March 31, 2022."

Without retrieval, the model will fallback to generic textbook knowledge: typical risk factors, generic explanations of rate decisions, and stylized facts about market reactions. That may be pedagogically interesting, but it is not sufficient for serious analysis, backtesting, or compliance-sensitive workflows.

Retrieval solves this by giving the model precise, context-specific information at run time. Temporal retrieval then ensures that this information respects the time dimension that markets live in.

Building the Retrieval-Augmented Generation Pipeline

A RAG system for financial analysis follows a series of stages. Understanding each stage conceptually will help you design and debug your own pipeline.

Defining Your Document Corpora

First, you select what sources you want the autonomous analyst to have access to. Common corpora include:

- **Corporate disclosures**: 10-Ks, 10-Qs, 20-Fs, annual reports, earnings call transcripts, investor day presentations.
- **Macro and policy documents**: FOMC minutes and statements, inflation reports, central bank speeches, fiscal policy announcements.
- **Research and commentary**: internal research notes, broker reports (subject to licensing), strategy pieces, factor reports.

- **Trading and risk logs**: daily P&L notes, risk committee minutes, trade rationales, execution reports.

Think of this as defining the "reading room" your analyst can consult. The better your corpora, the richer and more grounded the analysis.

Chunking into Semantically Coherent Units

Documents are often long: a 10-K can run to hundreds of pages. Feeding an entire filing to the model for every query is wasteful and can clutter the context with irrelevant details. Instead, we split documents into smaller "chunks" that still make sense on their own.

For example:

- For 10-Ks, chunk by section (e.g., "Business Overview," "Risk Factors," "MD&A") and sub-sections.
- For earnings calls, chunk by speaker turns or small groups of turns ("Analyst Q&A," "Prepared remarks on guidance").
- For research notes, chunk by logical paragraphs or headings.

The goal is to make each chunk a small, coherent piece of information: one idea, one topic, or one answer to a question. This makes retrieval more precise and context windows more efficient.

Encoding and Indexing with Embeddings and Metadata

Once we have chunks, we convert them into a form we can search. Modern retrieval systems typically use *embeddings*—numerical vectors that capture semantic meaning. Chunks with similar content end up close to each other in this vector space.

However, for financial applications, embeddings alone are not enough. We also attach metadata to each chunk, such as:

- **Ticker or instrument**: which company or asset it refers to.
- **Document type**: 10-K, earnings transcript, FOMC statement, research note, etc.
- **Publication date**: when the document became public.

- **Event date**: the date of the earnings call, meeting, or event described.
- **Effective-from / effective-to**: for information that is valid over a range of dates (e.g., a policy regime).

We then store both the embedding and the metadata in a *vector store* or similar index so that we can search by meaning and filter by structured attributes.

Retrieval with Semantic Search and Filters

When a query arrives—say, "What risks did JPM highlight around its investment banking revenues in the last three annual reports?"—we:

- Encode the query into an embedding.
- Use that embedding to retrieve candidate chunks that are semantically similar (e.g., risk factor sections mentioning investment banking).
- Apply metadata filters: ticker = JPM, document type in {10-K, annual report}, publication date in a specified range.

This combination of semantic search plus filters is called *hybrid retrieval*. It ensures that we find chunks that are both topically relevant and contextually appropriate (right company, right document type, right time period).

Reranking and Context Shaping

The initial retrieval step usually returns more chunks than we can reasonably feed to the model. We need a second pass that:

- Scores each chunk by a combination of semantic similarity and financial relevance (e.g., giving extra weight to primary sources like official filings).
- Prioritizes more recent or time-relevant chunks (e.g., the last two 10-Ks rather than a 10-year-old filing).
- Ensures diversity so that we do not give the model ten near-identical passages.

We then select the top-k chunks and arrange them into a context block that is passed to the LLM alongside the user's question and any system or task prompts.

This context shaping stage is where you can implement domain-specific heuristics. For example:

- For earnings questions, always include the last two quarters' transcripts and guidance sections first.
- For macro questions, always include the most recent policy statement and minutes, plus a small selection of prior ones for comparison.
- For risk scenario questions, include both internal risk reports and external news coverage for the event window.

Temporal Retrieval: Respecting the Information Set

So far we have described a standard RAG system. In markets, we must go further and make retrieval *time-aware*. The key idea is simple:

> When simulating a decision at time T, the analyst must not use information that became available after T.

Violating this rule leads to "look-ahead bias," which can make trading strategies and risk processes look much better in backtests than they would have been in reality.

Indexing with Dates and Horizons

Temporal retrieval starts with careful indexing. For each document and chunk, we should store:

- **Publication timestamp**: when the document was released.
- **Event date**: when the underlying event occurred (e.g., earnings date, meeting date).

- **Effective-from / effective-to dates** for information that spans a period (e.g., a tax regime or policy framework).

When a query includes an as-of date (for example, "as of 2022-03-31"), we restrict retrieval to documents whose publication date is less than or equal to that as-of date, and whose effective period includes it where relevant.

This means that if you ask, "What did we know about this company's leverage profile as of March 2022?" the analyst will not accidentally use the 2023 10-K or a 2024 research report.

Temporal Filters and Event Windows

In many analyses we care about a window around an event. For instance:

- Market reaction to earnings: event date D, window $[D-5, D+5]$ trading days.
- Policy shock analysis: window around a rate decision or unexpected data release.

Temporal filters let you express such windows at the retrieval stage. Instead of searching the entire corpus, you search only those chunks whose timestamps fall in the relevant interval, or that explicitly reference that event.

This has two benefits:

- It prevents contamination by future narratives (e.g., later post-mortems of the event).
- It focuses the model on contemporaneous information—the same information real traders had when they were reacting.

"State as of Date T" Queries

A powerful use case for temporal retrieval is reconstructing the information set at a past date:

> "Assume we are at 2020-02-15. Based only on information available up to that date, what were the main known risks around global supply chains?"

To support this, your retrieval layer must:

- Accept an explicit as-of date parameter.
- Restrict all document retrieval to items with publication date $\leq$ as-of date.
- Optionally differentiate between "public information" (e.g., filings, news) and "internal information" (e.g., your firm's research notes), depending on what scenario you are simulating.

The LLM then synthesizes a narrative grounded only in that filtered context. This is invaluable for:

- Counterfactual analysis ("Given what we knew then, was the trade reasonable?").
- Policy reviews and risk committee post-mortems.
- Backtesting "narrative-aware" strategies that depend on the news flow or research coverage at the time.

Designing Time-Aware Retrieval Chains for Common Workflows

Let us make these ideas concrete by sketching a few retrieval "chains" tailored to typical financial tasks.

Earnings Question Chain

For a query like "How has AAPL's guidance on gross margin evolved over the last year?", a time-aware chain might:

- Parse the ticker (AAPL) and relevant time horizon (last 4 quarters).

- Retrieve and chunk the last four earnings call transcripts and associated slide decks.
- Filter chunks to those whose section or text mentions "guidance" and "gross margin."
- Rerank chunks to emphasize prepared remarks from management over analyst Q&A, and the most recent quarters over older ones.
- Feed the top chunks into the LLM with a task prompt that asks for a structured summary of guidance level, direction of change, and key drivers.

If you are simulating an analyst's view as of a specific quarter, you additionally ensure that later quarters' documents are excluded by publication date.

Macro Narrative Chain

For a macro question like "Explain the shift in market expectations for Fed policy during Q1 2025," the chain could:

- Take the time window (Q1 2025) as a constraint.
- Retrieve FOMC statements, minutes, and key Fed speeches released during that quarter.
- Retrieve major macro data releases for that window (inflation, employment, growth).
- Retrieve internal or external strategy notes that reacted to those events, labeling them as "commentary" rather than primary sources.
- Rerank so that primary sources and a small set of representative commentaries dominate the context.

The LLM is then asked to reconstruct a time-ordered narrative: what the Fed said, what data came out, how expectations shifted, and what risks were highlighted at the time.

Keeping the Model Honest, Current, and Causally Consistent

A well-designed RAG and temporal retrieval system changes the role of the LLM in your architecture:

- Instead of being the *source* of factual market knowledge, it becomes a *user* of your factual sources.
- Instead of free-associating from its training data, it is constrained to reason over the specific documents and data you retrieve.
- Instead of accidentally seeing the future in historical analyses, it is limited to the information set available at each point in time.

To make this work in practice, you should:

- Treat RAG as a first-class subsystem, not an afterthought tacked onto prompts.
- Invest in thoughtful document ingestion, chunking, and metadata design.
- Always pass explicit as-of dates and horizons into your retrieval layer for backtests and scenario reconstructions.
- Log not just the final answers but also the retrieved documents and timestamps for each question, so you can audit and improve the system.

By grounding the autonomous analyst in relevant, time-aware information, you close the gap between clever text generation and serious financial analysis. In the final section, we will assemble these ingredients—prompting, function calling, and time-aware retrieval—into full agentic workflows that can run complete market investigations with limited human intervention.

5.3 Structured Extraction and Agent Orchestration

In the first two sections of this chapter we gave the autonomous analyst three core abilities: (i) to follow precise prompts and call tools deterministically, and (ii) to ground its reasoning in retrieved, time-aware information rather than its frozen training set. We now assemble these ingredients into full *workflows* that can run substantial parts of a market analysis with limited human intervention.

There are three pillars:

- **Structured extraction**: asking the model to produce machine-usable outputs (fields, tags, tables) rather than free-form essays.
- **Memory**: deciding what the analyst should remember (and for how long) so that it can build on prior work without becoming confused or leaking sensitive data.
- **Agent orchestration**: coordinating multiple specialized "sub-analysts" and tools into multi-step chains that resemble how a real research team operates.

By the end of this section, you should be able to turn high-level tasks such as "Explain the drivers of last week's move in European banks and flag risks to our portfolio" into reproducible agent workflows: retrieve data and documents, extract structured facts, run analytics, synthesize a view, and subject that view to a basic risk review.

Why Structured Extraction Matters

Large language models are naturally good at prose: they can write convincing paragraphs about almost anything. For production trading systems, however, prose alone is not enough. You need outputs that:

- Can be parsed and stored in databases.
- Can be used as inputs to backtests and risk engines.

- Are easy to compare across time, assets, and teams.

This is the role of *structured extraction*: we ask the model to read messy inputs—earnings calls, strategy notes, news flows—and distill them into explicit, well-defined fields.

A few typical examples:

- Extracting from an earnings call, for each line of analyst Q&A: sentiment (positive/negative/neutral), topic (pricing, volume, costs, regulation), and whether guidance was reaffirmed or changed.
- Reading a long macro commentary and pulling out a structured risk narrative: key macro themes, probabilities attached to scenarios, assets expected to be most sensitive.
- Parsing a daily P&L note to tag each loss as "idiosyncratic," "sector-wide," or "macro," and linking each to a reference event.

Once you have structure, you can aggregate, visualize, and backtest. For example, you can test whether earnings calls with a high density of "cost pressure" remarks historically led to downward margin revisions.

Designing Schemas for Financial Extraction

The foundation of structured extraction is the *schema*: a description of the fields you want, their types, and how they relate to each other. A good schema for financial work is:

- **Minimal but complete**: only fields you will actually use, but enough to support your downstream questions.
- **Stable**: rarely changing, so you can compare outputs across time.
- **Clear**: with unambiguous definitions you can explain to a colleague.

Consider a schema for line-level earnings call analysis. For each speaker turn we might define:

- speaker_role: one of {"management", "analyst", "moderator"}.
- topic: short string from a controlled vocabulary (e.g., "revenue", "margins", "capex", "regulation", "guidance").
- sentiment: one of {"negative", "neutral", "positive"}.
- surprise_vs_consensus: one of {"worse", "in_line", "better", "not_applicable"}.
- forward_looking: boolean indicating whether the statement is about the future.

In your prompts, you:

- Describe the schema in plain language.
- Provide one or two annotated examples (few-shot prompting).
- Ask the model to return a structured object (for example, a list of records), not narrative prose.

You can then run simple checks: does every turn have a topic? Are there only known sentiment values? Any violations trigger a retry or a correction step.

Error Handling and Validation in Extraction

No extraction system is perfect on the first try. Robust workflows assume that the model will sometimes:

- Omit required fields.
- Use values outside the allowed set.
- Misinterpret ambiguous text.

You can handle these issues with a thin validation and retry layer:

- **Syntactic validation**: check that the output parses (for instance, valid JSON) and all required top-level fields are present.
- **Type and range validation**: ensure that numeric fields are numbers, enumerations are from allowed lists, and strings meet length limits.
- **Semantic spot-checks**: for critical tasks, compare a subset of fields to known values or to a second model run.

When a check fails, you respond to the model with a concise correction prompt: "Your previous output omitted the field surprise_vs_consensus on some items. Please correct and return a new version that includes this field on every record."

This pattern—*model output → validation → feedback → refinement*—turns the LLM into a cooperative component that can be steered toward high-quality structured data.

Combining Structured Extraction with Tool Use

Structured extraction becomes particularly powerful when paired with tools and retrieval. A typical pattern for an earnings workflow might be:

- Use retrieval to pull the latest earnings transcript and associated slides for a given ticker.
- Call a text-splitting function to break the transcript into manageable speaker turns.
- Ask the model to perform structured extraction on each turn according to an agreed schema.
- Aggregate the results with a separate tool (for example, count how many negative comments about "demand" occurred in the last 15 minutes of the call).

- Store both the raw extraction and the aggregated metrics in your research database.

The LLM sits at the center, orchestrating these steps: it decides which tools to call, applies the schema, and interprets the outputs. The combination of deterministic tools and structured formats makes the resulting pipeline reproducible and auditable.

From a Single Analyst to a Team of Agents

Up to this point we have mostly described a single, general-purpose analyst using tools and retrieval. In many real workflows, however, you implicitly imagine a *team*:

- Someone fetches the data and documents.
- Someone else extracts structured features.
- A senior analyst interprets the features in context.
- A risk officer reviews the proposal and highlights blind spots.

Agent orchestration is about making this implicit team explicit in your system design. You define specialized sub-agents, each with its own role, prompts, tools, and sometimes its own memory:

- A **Data Retriever** agent, tuned for RAG and temporal constraints.
- A **Structured Extractor** agent, optimized for schema adherence.
- A **Fundamental or Macro Analyst** agent, responsible for synthesizing narratives and linking to economic logic.
- A **Risk Reviewer** agent, tasked with adversarially probing assumptions and flagging risks.

These agents are coordinated by a lightweight **Controller** that decides the sequence of steps, passes intermediate results from one agent to another, and collects the final answer.

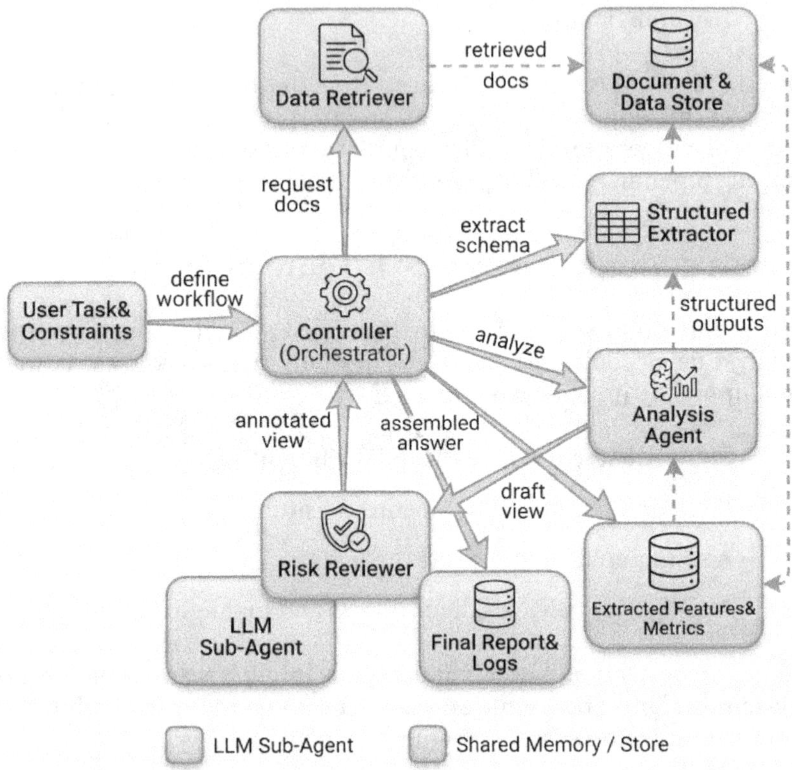

Orchestration Patterns: Chains, Branches, and Loops

With specialized agents in place, we can choose different orchestration patterns depending on the task.

Sequential Chains

The simplest pattern is a *chain*: a fixed sequence of steps where the output of one agent feeds directly into the next. For example, a daily equity event analysis chain:

- **Retriever**: given a ticker and date, gather relevant filings, news, and intraday price data for the last 48 hours.

- **Extractor**: from those documents, extract key events (earnings, guidance changes, rating changes) and their properties (direction, magnitude, theme).
- **Analysis agent**: explain the price move using the extracted events plus price and volume data.
- **Risk reviewer**: highlight missing angles, correlated exposures, or model limitations.

Sequential chains are easy to reason about, test, and log, making them a good starting point.

Branching Workflows

Many analyses break naturally into parallel branches. Suppose you want a sector-level view that aggregates company-level extractions. A branching workflow might:

- Use the controller to split the sector universe into subsets (for example, by market cap or region).
- For each subset, launch a parallel chain: retrieve documents for each name, extract structured events, and compute summary metrics.
- Merge the outputs at the end into a sector dashboard.

The controller does not need to be complex; it can simply keep track of which branches have finished and then trigger a consolidation step.

Iterative Refinement Loops

Finally, some tasks benefit from *iterative refinement*. For instance, when the risk reviewer finds gaps in the initial analysis, it can trigger a loop:

- The analysis agent produces a draft view.
- The risk reviewer critiques it: "You did not consider FX exposure" or "You relied only on our internal research, not on filings."

- The controller passes this critique back to the analysis agent (and possibly the retriever), asking for targeted additional retrieval and revised analysis.
- The cycle repeats until either a stopping criterion is met (for example, no major new risks identified) or a resource limit is reached.

These loops mimic the real-world back-and-forth between analysts and risk teams, but at machine speed and across many assets.

Memory: What the Analyst Should Remember

Orchestrated agents need memory to be effective. But "memory" in this context is not mystical; it is simply the collection of states and logs your system retains across steps and over time. It is helpful to distinguish two levels:

- **Short-term memory**: context that lives for the duration of a single workflow or conversation.
- **Long-term memory**: durable records that persist across days, weeks, or months.

Short-Term Memory: Within a Workflow

Within a single analysis run (for instance, "Explain today's move in AAPL"), the controller maintains:

- The user's task specification and constraints (universe, as-of date, risk budget).
- The sequence of tool calls and agent outputs.
- Shared scratchpads: extracted events, computed metrics, partial narratives.

This short-term memory allows agents to build on each other without having to re-derive everything from scratch. Technically, it may be represented as an evolving state object that is passed as input to each agent's prompt, often summarized to fit context limits.

Long-Term Memory: Across Workflows

Long-term memory is where you store:

- Extracted facts: line-level earnings tags, macro event annotations, risk narratives.
- Derived metrics: factor exposures, sentiment indices, macro regime labels.
- Past decisions and rationales: what trades were considered or made, and why.

This information is not just for human review. It can be fed back into retrieval as part of your RAG corpora, so that future analyses can reference past insights. For example, when analyzing a new earnings call, the analyst might recall: "In the last three quarters, management repeatedly emphasized FX headwinds."

You must, however, manage privacy and scope:

- Not all long-term memory is available to all workflows; some may be desk-specific or strategy-specific.
- For compliance reasons, certain data (for example, client details) should never appear in prompts at all.

In practice, long-term memory is implemented through your existing storage systems: databases, document stores, vector indexes, and logging systems—now enriched by structured extraction.

Production Concerns: Caching, Guardrails, and Observability

As your workflows mature, operational details become central to reliability and cost.

Caching and Reuse

Many steps in an agentic pipeline are naturally cacheable:

- Once you have extracted structured fields from a 10-K, you rarely need to re-run that extraction unless your schema changes.
- Price history and factor exposures for a given as-of date and horizon can be cached and re-used across analyses.

By caching tool outputs and extracted features, you:

- Reduce latency for frequent queries.
- Lower your API and computation costs.
- Make workflows more deterministic, since the same underlying data are re-used.

The controller can check caches before issuing new tool calls, turning your analyst into a smart re-user of prior work.

Guardrails Around Sensitive Actions

Although earlier sections already emphasized risk limits in tools, agent orchestration adds another layer of control. You can:

- Restrict which agents are allowed to call which tools (for example, only a dedicated "Execution Simulator" agent can call simulated order APIs, and no one can call live execution).
- Insert "approval gates" in workflows: certain actions (for example, generating a trade recommendation) only proceed if a human approves or if automated checks pass.
- Configure different policies by environment: more permissive in research sandboxes, stricter in production.

These guardrails are enforced not only by prompts but also by the surrounding system: agents simply cannot see tools they are not allowed to use.

Observability and Post-Mortem Prompts

Finally, to trust an autonomous analyst, you need to understand *why* it did what it did. Good observability includes:

- Logging all prompts and responses for each agent, along with tool calls and their results.
- Storing retrieved documents and their timestamps for each analysis.
- Recording key decisions by the controller (for example, which branches were taken, why loops were terminated).

On top of raw logs, you can use the model itself for "post-mortem" explanations. After a workflow completes, you might ask a specialized explanation agent:

> "Given the full trace of this analysis, describe the main steps the system took, the key data it relied on, and any limitations or potential sources of error."

This produces an audit-friendly narrative you can share with risk committees, model validation teams, or regulators.

From Workflows to an Evolving Research Platform

Putting everything together, the autonomous analyst is no longer a single model sitting behind a chat interface. It is a *research platform* composed of:

- Carefully designed prompts and function-calling interfaces.
- RAG pipelines that provide timely, causally consistent information.
- Structured extraction schemas that turn text into data.
- Orchestrated agents that mirror the division of labor in real research teams.
- Memory and logging systems that accumulate knowledge and support audit.

As you deploy these workflows across more tasks and asset classes, you will refine schemas, add or retire tools, and adjust orchestration patterns. The aim is not to replace human judgment, but to automate the repetitive, mechanical parts of market analysis, so that human experts can focus on designing strategies, interpreting edge cases, and deciding when to act.

Done well, this combination of structured extraction, memory, and agent orchestration moves the autonomous analyst from an impressive demo to a dependable part of your trading and investment infrastructure.

Chapter 6

Quant Applications and Portfolio Execution

This chapter shows how to turn raw language-model insights into actual P&L. We'll start by transforming messy news and social chatter into time-stamped sentiment curves, then layer in event and filings analysis that can explain-and sometimes anticipate-price moves. Finally, we'll walk through how these signals feed a portfolio engine that respects risk, liquidity, and execution costs, so the outputs of your autonomous analyst become trades that can really be put on in the market.

6.1 Sentiment, News, and Event-Driven Signals

In earlier chapters we treated LLMs mainly as powerful encoders of text: they turned documents into numerical representations or extracted structured fields that could be merged with traditional datasets. We now move one step closer to trading.

This section focuses on building an end-to-end pipeline that starts from raw information flow—news headlines, social media posts, earnings call transcripts—and ends with a clean, time-aligned panel of tradable sentiment and event-driven signals. Along the way we must solve three practical problems:

- Ingest heterogeneous text streams and align them to a common market clock and ticker universe.
- Use LLMs to convert each document into structured scores: directional sentiment, surprise, relevance, and event type.
- Model how prices typically react, both immediately and with drift, around the events implied by those texts.

The goal is not just to "have sentiment" but to engineer a robust, backtest-ready factor that can sit beside classic signals such as value, momentum, and quality.

From Raw Text to a Market-Aligned Data Stream

Market text arrives in many forms and with varying structure:

- Newswire headlines and articles with timestamps and tickers, but also many irrelevant or duplicated stories.
- Social media posts that are short, noisy, and often ambiguous in ticker references.
- Long-form transcripts and research reports that are rich in information but slow to arrive and slow to process.

Before we can exploit LLM capabilities, we must normalize these feeds and connect them to the same axes as our price data: instrument, time, and (optionally) market venue.

Data ingestion and timestamping

At ingestion time, each document should be mapped to a minimal schema:

- **Raw text:** the headline, body, or transcript segment.
- **Source metadata:** provider, language, feed type (news, social, transcript).
- **Publication timestamp:** as provided by the source.
- **Received timestamp:** when it first appears in your system.

The distinction between publication and received times is crucial. In backtests, using publication time when you would only have seen the news with a delay leads to look-ahead bias. For real trading we care about the earliest time we could plausibly react, which is closer to the received time, plus any processing latency.

A simple but effective rule is:

- Use the *received* timestamp as the time at which the sentiment becomes tradable.
- Track the lag between publication and receipt for each source and monitor changes over time.

Ticker and entity resolution

Next, each piece of text must be linked to one or more instruments:

- News stories often carry explicit tickers; you can accept these, but still run a consistency check using named-entity recognition (NER) on company names.
- Social posts may reference tickers (e.g., $AAPL) or company names, or even colloquial nicknames.
- Macro news (e.g., CPI releases) may have no ticker, but affect indices, sectors, or asset classes.

LLMs can assist here in two ways:

- **NER + linking:** A small prompt asks the model to list all public companies, indices, or macro entities mentioned. This is especially helpful for messy social text.

- **Relevance classification:** For each candidate ticker (e.g., inferred by keyword search), the LLM judges whether the document is truly about that ticker or only mentions it peripherally.

The output of this stage is a stream of *document–instrument* pairs: each document linked to the set of instruments for which it is potentially informative.

Aligning to the market clock

Financial time series are usually sampled on a regular grid: minute bars, five-minute bars, or daily closes. Text events are irregular. To integrate them, you must:

- Choose a base time resolution (for example, one minute for intraday strategies, or one day for slower strategies).
- For each document, map its tradable time (received timestamp plus latency) to the corresponding bar index.

At this point you can imagine a large panel indexed by $(\text{time}, \text{instrument})$. Initially, this panel is empty on most cells: at each time and for each instrument, there may be zero, one, or many associated documents. The rest of the pipeline will fill this panel with sentiment scores and event flags.

LLM-Based Scoring: Sentiment, Surprise, and Relevance

With a clean stream of document–instrument pairs and their aligned timestamps, we can design LLM prompts and classifier heads to extract useful signals. Conceptually, each document is transformed into a small vector of scores:

$$\text{scores} = (\text{sentiment}, \text{magnitude}, \text{surprise}, \text{topic}, \text{event type}, \dots)$$

We want these scores to have intuitive meanings and to be comparable across sources and over time.

Directional sentiment and strength

Directional sentiment is the backbone of many text-driven strategies: is this document good or bad for the future return of the instrument?

A practical design is to ask the LLM two related questions:

- *Direction:* On a scale from -1 (very negative) to $+1$ (very positive), what is the expected effect of this news on the stock price over the next one trading day?
- *Confidence or magnitude:* How strong is this effect, on a scale from 0 (negligible) to 1 (very strong)?

By asking about *expected price impact* rather than generic tone, you encourage the model to focus on materiality. A polite but economically disastrous announcement (e.g., a large equity dilution) should still receive a strongly negative score.

From these answers you can build a numeric sentiment factor, for example:

$$S_{d,i} = \text{direction}_{d,i} \times \text{magnitude}_{d,i}$$

for document d and instrument i.

Surprise versus consensus

Markets care about surprises: information that is different from what was expected. LLMs can help approximate this even when you do not have a full numeric consensus dataset handy.

For earnings-related text, you might ask:

- Did the company's results appear better, in line with, or worse than what analysts and investors were likely expecting?
- Is the guidance stronger, in line, or weaker than prior guidance and typical market expectations?

Responses can be mapped to a discrete variable (e.g., -1, 0, $+1$) or a more granular scale. For macro news, similar prompts can reference "market expectations" or "consensus estimates."

Surprise scores often complement raw sentiment: a neutral-toned press release that signals a large positive surprise (e.g., much stronger margins than usual) may be more tradable than an effusive but expected success.

Topic and event-type classification

Not all news items are equally relevant to your strategy. It is helpful to have the LLM classify documents into:

- **Topic buckets:** macro, sector trends, company fundamentals, regulation, ESG, etc.
- **Event types:** earnings result, guidance change, M&A announcement, product launch, regulatory investigation, macro print, and so on.

These labels serve multiple purposes:

- They allow you to filter out news types you do not wish to trade.
- They allow you to run event studies by category: you can estimate how earnings surprises differ from regulatory shocks.
- They facilitate risk management by separating stock-specific from market-wide events.

From an implementation perspective, you can either use direct prompting ("Classify this document into one of the following event types..."), or train lightweight classifier heads on top of LLM embeddings if you have labeled data.

Aggregating Documents into Time-Series Sentiment Factors

Documents are sparse and noisy. A single tweet or headline may be mis-scored, duplicated, or irrelevant. Portfolio construction prefers smoother, more robust factors. We therefore aggregate the document-level scores into time-series features at the (time, instrument) level.

Within-bar aggregation

Within a single time bar (say, one minute), an instrument may be associated with multiple documents across different sources. You can aggregate document scores $S_{d,i}$ into a bar-level sentiment $S_{t,i}$ with rules such as:

- **Weighted average:** weight by source reliability or by the model's confidence.
- **Max-abs rule:** keep the most extreme sentiment in magnitude, which captures the strongest signal at that instant.
- **Source diversification:** compute separate aggregates for news, social, and transcripts, then blend them with fixed or learned weights.

You may also want to deduplicate near-identical headlines that arrive within seconds of each other from different providers. Textual similarity (using embeddings) and shared URLs or IDs can be used to cluster and downweight duplicates.

Rolling windows and decay

For intraday trading, the information content of a news item decays over time. For daily or weekly horizons, some news may keep influencing returns for several days.

A simple way to model this is with an exponential decay:

$$\tilde{S}_{t,i} = \sum_{\tau \le t} S_{\tau,i} \cdot \exp\left(-\frac{t-\tau}{\lambda}\right)$$

where λ is the decay parameter measured in bars or days. Intuitively, recent sentiment has higher weight, but past news still contributes for some time.

Rather than hard-coding λ, you can:

- Estimate the decay empirically via event studies (see below), or
- Treat the decayed sentiment measures at different λ values as candidate features and let downstream forecasting models learn their relative importance.

At the end of aggregation, you have one or more sentiment factors per instrument and time bar, ready to be merged with price and volume data:

$$\text{panel: } S_{t,i}^{(k)}, \quad k = 1, \ldots, K$$

for example, "news sentiment," "social sentiment," and "earnings-transcript sentiment," each with its own decay structure.

Event Detection and Event Windows

So far we have focused on a continuous stream of text-driven sentiment. Many profitable patterns, however, revolve around *discrete events*: earnings releases, guidance cuts, M&A announcements, regulatory actions, and macro data prints.

LLMs help us identify and characterize these events automatically.

Detecting events from text

Using the event-type classification discussed earlier, you can flag documents that indicate the start of an event. For example:

- An earnings event begins when the first document that clearly conveys the earnings result appears.
- An M&A event begins when the first reliable report of a deal, rumor, or strategic review is published.
- A macro event begins when the official release text or a reliable summary hits the wires.

To avoid double-counting, cluster documents that refer to the same underlying event:

- For earnings, cluster by ticker and fiscal period within a short time window.
- For M&A, cluster by acquirer–target pairs.
- For macro, cluster by release name and date.

LLMs can assist in clustering by normalizing event descriptions (for example, turning varied descriptions of a "Q2 2027 earnings call" into a canonical label).

Defining event windows

Once events are identified, we define event windows: time intervals around the event during which we study price behavior. For example:

- $[-30\,\text{min}, +120\,\text{min}]$ around intraday earnings announcements.
- $[0, +5\,\text{days}]$ after daily macro releases.

For each event e and associated instrument i, we can compute:

- *Raw returns*: the cumulative return over the event window.
- *Abnormal returns*: returns minus a benchmark, such as a factor model or index.

These event windows provide the empirical grounding for our sentiment factors. They allow us to ask: when the LLM judged an event to be highly negative and surprising, what actually happened to the stock price, on average?

Modeling Immediate Reactions and Post-Event Drift

Markets typically respond to news in two phases:

- **Immediate reaction:** a jump or rapid move as information is incorporated.
- **Post-event drift:** a slower tendency for prices to continue moving in the same direction (or overreact and mean-revert) over hours or days.

Understanding these patterns is essential to designing viable trading strategies. LLM-derived sentiment and surprise scores give us a natural way to condition on event characteristics.

Estimating event-study alphas

For each event, we can summarize its LLM scores into a few key variables:

- S_e: signed sentiment (negative to positive).
- U_e: surprise relative to expectations (e.g., worse than, in-line, better than).
- T_e: event type (earnings, guidance, M&A, regulatory, macro).

We then estimate average abnormal returns conditional on these variables. For example:

- High positive sentiment and positive surprise earnings events.
- High negative sentiment regulatory events.

For each group, compute:

- The average abnormal return in the first bar or first day (immediate reaction).

- The cumulative abnormal return over follow-up windows (e.g., day 2–5).

These averages, often called event-study alphas, inform:

- Which combinations of sentiment and event type produce reliably directional trades.
- How long it usually takes for the price response to play out.

Decay and half-life of impact

To quantify drift-style effects, we can look at the time profile of average abnormal returns following an event. A common observation is:

- A large portion of the move happens quickly, then the incremental effect decays over time.

By fitting a simple decaying pattern to the cumulative abnormal return curve, you can estimate a half-life: the time it takes for the marginal impact of the event to fall by half. This half-life can guide:

- The holding period of an event-driven position.
- The decay parameter used when constructing continuous sentiment factors.

Different event types and sentiment strengths may have different half-lives. LLM-based event labels make it straightforward to segment by these categories.

Practical Pitfalls and Robustness Checks

Building sentiment and event-driven signals is as much about filtering and debiasing as it is about modeling. Here are some practical considerations.

Media attention and selection bias

Popular, large-cap stocks generate more news and social chatter than small, illiquid names. If you simply trade on raw sentiment, you might unintentionally tilt toward high-attention stocks or sectors.

To mitigate this:

- Normalize sentiment by the typical volume of news for that stock (e.g., today's sentiment versus a rolling baseline).
- Include controls for size and trading activity when evaluating performance.

Market-wide versus idiosyncratic news

Macro or sector-wide news can move many stocks simultaneously. If your sentiment signal is really capturing market-wide shocks, you may be double-counting risk factors you already model elsewhere.

Using the LLM's topic and event-type labels, you can:

- Separate market-wide from stock-specific events.
- In event studies, compare a stock's response to that of its sector or factor peers, to isolate idiosyncratic components.

Robustness via subsamples and exclusions

A good test of any signal is whether its performance persists after removing the strongest, most obvious cases. For example:

- Re-run event studies excluding the top 5% most extreme sentiment events; see if the pattern survives.
- Test performance in periods of high and low volatility separately.
- Shuffle sentiment labels (or use time-shifted sentiment) to create a placebo benchmark.

If your sentiment factor's edge disappears once you remove a tiny set of spectacular events, it may be fragile or overly tuned.

From Sentiment Factors to Portfolio Inputs

By the end of this process, you have moved from raw, heterogeneous text streams to structured, time-aligned signals:

- Continuous sentiment factors for each instrument and time bar.
- Discrete event flags with associated LLM-derived features (sentiment, surprise, event type).
- Empirical estimates of how prices typically react around those events.

In the next section, these signals become inputs to forecasting models and portfolio optimizers. There, we will connect a cross-section of expected returns—partly driven by the text signals described here—to position sizes, risk budgets, and execution tactics.

Before turning to portfolio construction, it is helpful to visualize the entire pipeline that carries information from raw text to tradable signals.

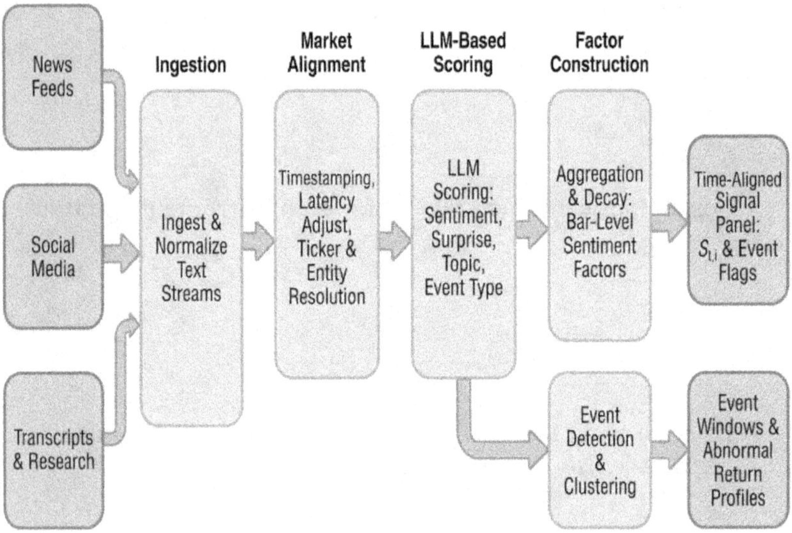

6.2 Filings Analysis and Signal Fusion with Time Series

In the previous section we transformed fast, fragmentary information streams—news, social media, transcripts—into time-aligned sentiment and event signals. Those signals tend to be short-lived and highly reactive. We now turn to a slower, deeper layer of information: formal corporate disclosures such as 10-Ks, 10-Qs, annual reports, and full earnings call transcripts.

These documents are long, technical, and dense with nuance about strategy, risks, and accounting choices. They are also relatively infrequent: a typical firm files a 10-K once a year and 10-Qs each quarter. This makes them a natural complement to high-frequency text signals. LLMs are particularly well suited here, because they can read and reason over long contexts in a way that traditional keyword-based methods cannot.

In this section we will:

- Build an LLM-based pipeline to read long-form disclosures and extract concrete, machine-usable features.
- Distinguish between point-in-time features (what this filing says today) and longitudinal features (how the language has changed over time).
- Fuse these text-derived features with numerical time-series predictors—prices, fundamentals, analyst estimates—to build forecasting models.
- Emphasize interpretability, so that every forecast or alpha signal can be traced back to specific passages in the underlying documents.

The end result is a set of richer, more stable forecasting models in which text and numbers work together.

Why Filings Matter for an Autonomous Analyst

Regulated filings and official reports play a special role in public markets:

- They are **legally constrained**. Companies must disclose certain information and are accountable for misstatements.
- They are **structured in format but unstructured in language**. Sections like "Management's Discussion and Analysis" (MD&A) and "Risk Factors" are standardized in position but not in wording.

- They reveal the firm's **narrative**: management's explanation of performance, forward-looking plans, and perceived risks.

Traditional quant signals often make limited use of these texts, focusing instead on the associated numeric fields (revenues, margins, leverage) and analyst estimate revisions. LLMs allow the autonomous analyst to bring the narrative itself into the modeling pipeline as a first-class data source.

A concrete goal is to move from the vague idea that "the tone of the 10-K seemed more cautious this year" to a quantifiable feature such as:

> "Risk disclosure tone was 2 standard deviations more negative than the firm's own five-year history, controlling for industry."

Segmenting and Retrieving Relevant Passages

Long-form disclosures can easily exceed hundreds of pages. Even a powerful LLM will be more accurate and efficient if we focus it on the most relevant sections.

Basic document segmentation

Most filings follow a semi-standard structure. For a 10-K, for example, you will typically find:

- *Business overview*
- *Risk factors*
- *Management's Discussion and Analysis* (MD&A)
- *Financial statements* and footnotes

A simple first step is to parse the document into sections by headings and store each section separately with metadata:

- filing type (10-K, 10-Q, etc.)
- company identifier

- filing date
- section type (MD&A, risk factors, notes, etc.)

Earnings call transcripts can be segmented into:

- prepared remarks by management
- Q&A with analysts

This already provides a coarse way to aim the LLM: for example, use MD&A to understand recent performance drivers, risk factors to understand tail risks, and Q&A to capture off-script insights.

Retrieval-augmented focus

Within each section, not every paragraph is equally informative. Rather than asking the LLM to read entire sections at once, we can use retrieval techniques to pull out the most relevant passages for a given task.

For example, suppose we want to assess management's stance on capital allocation. We can:

- Embed all paragraphs using an embedding model.
- Define a set of query vectors representing topics such as "share repurchases", "dividends", "M&A strategy", "debt reduction".
- Retrieve the top paragraphs most similar to these queries.

We then feed only these retrieved paragraphs into the LLM with a task-specific prompt (e.g., "Summarize management's capital allocation priorities over the next 12 months"). This retrieval-augmented step keeps the LLM's attention on the passages that matter for the signal we want to build.

Designing Machine-Usable Outputs from Filings

Once we have isolated relevant segments, the key design choice is: *what exactly do we want the LLM to output?* Vague summaries are not sufficient for systematic trading. We need structured, stable, and interpretable features.

Below are several useful categories.

Structured KPIs mentioned in text

Text often refers to key performance indicators (KPIs) that are not present as line items in the standardized financial statements. Examples include:

- number of active users
- churn rates
- same-store sales
- order backlog

LLM prompts can ask:

- Identify any KPIs that management highlights as important to the business model.
- For each KPI, extract the current value and, if discussed, its year-over-year or quarter-over-quarter change.

The outputs are small, structured records: KPI name, current value, reference period, change direction, and magnitude if available. These can be turned into time series and compared over time or across peers.

Forward-looking statements and guidance language

Management often provides qualitative or semi-quantitative guidance, such as "we expect revenue to grow in the low-teens percent range" or "we anticipate a modest decline in margins next quarter."

Here the tasks for the LLM may include:

- Extracting any explicit numerical guidance ranges and mapping them to numeric values (e.g., "low-teens" as 10–13%).
- Flagging the directional stance for key metrics: revenue, margins, capex, leverage, unit volumes.

These features can then be compared against realized outcomes or analyst estimates, producing guidance-accuracy or guidance-surprise measures over time.

Tone and emphasis in risk language

The "Risk Factors" and related sections can be particularly revealing when language shifts meaningfully from one filing to another. Useful LLM-derived features include:

- Overall tone: how negative, cautious, or urgent is the language about key risks?
- Emergence of new risks: does the filing introduce risk themes not present in previous years (e.g., cyber security, regulatory investigations, key supplier concentration)?
- Change in emphasis: does the filing spend more or less space on specific risk categories relative to its own history and to peers?

For each risk category, the LLM might output:

- a sentiment score (from very positive to very negative)
- an importance score (how central this risk is to the overall discussion)
- a novelty flag (new, expanded, unchanged, or reduced compared with the previous filing)

These outputs naturally lend themselves to longitudinal analysis.

Qualitative flags: management credibility and litigation overhang

Some signals are hard to quantify but still amenable to structured judgment. For example:

- Does management consistently acknowledge mistakes and uncertainty, or do they use overly promotional language?
- Is there ongoing or potential litigation that could materially affect the firm?

Carefully crafted prompts can ask the LLM to assign low-dimensional scores or categorical labels such as:

- management credibility: low / medium / high
- legal/regulatory overhang: none / moderate / significant

While these labels are somewhat subjective, they can be validated historically by checking, for example, whether "low credibility" firms are more likely to issue large negative surprises later or to underperform.

Point-in-Time Versus Longitudinal Features

Filings are episodic. For each filing date, we can compute a snapshot of all the above features. But much of the informational value lies in *how* these features evolve.

Point-in-time extraction

Point-in-time (PIT) features describe what the filing says at its release date:

- Current KPI levels and guidance.
- Current tone of risk language.
- Snapshot of management's capital allocation stance.

When merging PIT features with time-series data, it is crucial to assign them the correct timestamp (the filing release time) and to respect any delays in data availability (e.g., processing latency). As with news, we must avoid look-ahead bias by ensuring that a model trained at time t only sees filings that would have been available by that time in a live setting.

Longitudinal changes and surprises

Longitudinal features capture the *change* from one filing to the next, either for a given company or relative to a peer group. These are often more powerful than levels.

Examples include:

- Change in the negativity of risk language relative to the firm's own past.
- Appearance of new risk categories not previously mentioned.
- Widening or narrowing of guidance ranges.
- Shifts in emphasis between growth and profitability in management's narrative.

For each such feature, you can compute:

- A difference or percentage change from the prior filing.
- A standardized score relative to the firm's own historical distribution.
- A peer-relative score (e.g., how much more negative is this firm's risk tone compared to the sector median this year?).

This mirrors how we treat numeric fundamentals: both absolute levels and changes matter, but changes often drive price responses.

Aligning Text Features with Numerical Time Series

Once we have engineered a set of filing-based features, we need to fuse them with standard numerical predictors: prices, returns, accounting ratios, analyst estimate revisions, and alternative data. This requires careful alignment in both time and frequency.

Temporal alignment and feature lags

Filings arrive at irregular times (for example, quarterly). Numerical data, such as daily returns or monthly risk factors, are typically sampled on a regular grid. To combine them:

- Assign each filing-based feature to the date (and time) of the filing.

- Forward-fill or hold the latest filing feature constant until the next filing arrives, if appropriate for your horizon. For example, a change in risk factor language may influence investor perception for months.
- Alternatively, use explicit lagged versions of text features (e.g., one-quarter lag, two-quarter lag) as separate predictors.

The choice depends on the economic story. If you believe that a particular textual change has enduring implications for the firm's risk profile, a forward-filled representation is natural. If you are concerned about overlapping information and want to avoid look-ahead creeping in via forward-filling, you may instead work with discrete, event-style features and explicitly model the time since last filing.

Merging with cross-sectional and time-series predictors

On any modeling date, say the end of a month or quarter, your feature set might include:

- Standard cross-sectional predictors: valuation ratios, size, quality metrics, leverage.
- Time-series predictors: recent returns, volatility, momentum signals.
- Event- and sentiment-based features from the previous section.
- Filing-based textual features: PIT levels, longitudinal changes, and peer-relative scores.

The fusion is mostly mechanical: you join on instrument and date, ensuring that the textual features only use information known by that date. The main challenge is *dimensionality*: the number of potential text features can explode.

Managing Dimensionality: Regularization and Feature Compression

LLM-derived features can be high-dimensional. Even if each prompt outputs only a handful of scores, you may have dozens of prompts and multiple lags. To prevent overfitting, we must reduce and regularize.

Simple feature selection and grouping

A straightforward starting point is to group related features and construct composite indices. For example:

- Combine multiple risk-tone features into a "Risk Caution Index" for each firm.
- Combine different guidance-related features into a "Guidance Optimism Index."
- Summarize various litigation and regulatory flags into an "Overhang Score."

These indices can be averaged, or weighted according to expert judgment or simple cross-sectional regressions. The aim is to have a moderate number of interpretable features rather than a sprawling set of granular scores.

Regularized models

When you do want to keep a larger set of text features, regularization techniques such as Lasso (L1), Ridge (L2), or Elastic Net regressions can help prevent overfitting by shrinking or zeroing out less useful predictors.

From a practical perspective:

- Start with a relatively rich feature set, including various lags and interaction terms (e.g., interactions between textual risk tone and leverage).
- Fit a regularized model on a rolling or expanding window.
- Inspect which filing-based features consistently receive non-zero weights and whether they align with economic intuition.

This approach allows the model to discover which aspects of the text are truly informative while automatically discarding noisy signals.

Embedding-based compression

Another option is to represent entire filings or sections as dense vector embeddings and then compress those embeddings into a small number of principal components or factors. These components can be used directly as features.

While this approach is powerful, it can sacrifice some interpretability. A useful compromise is:

- Use embeddings primarily for retrieval and clustering (e.g., grouping firms with similar narratives).
- Use explicitly engineered LLM outputs (scores, labels, indices) for features that directly enter forecasting models.

Building Interpretable Forecasting Models

The ultimate aim is to produce forecasts of returns, risk, or other financial outcomes in which the contribution of filing-based text is both *statistically useful* and *explainable.*

Model choices

Many model families can accommodate fused text and numeric features:

- Linear cross-sectional regressions (e.g., predicting next-quarter returns from current features).
- Gradient boosting and random forests that can capture nonlinear interactions.
- Sequence models that take histories of both text and numeric features as input.

For a textbook setting and for interpretability, linear or generalized linear models are often a good starting point. They allow you to write down, for each instrument at each time, a predicted return as a weighted sum of features.

Tracing forecasts back to text

To keep the autonomous analyst auditable, any forecasting system that uses filing-derived features should support a "drill-down" workflow:

- For a given forecast on date t and instrument i, identify which features contributed most to the prediction (e.g., by absolute contribution in a linear model).
- For each key filing-based feature, retrieve:
  - the specific filing and section from which it was extracted,
  - the prompt that generated the feature, and
  - the underlying text snippet(s) provided to the LLM.
- Present this as an explanation, such as:

  > "The model's negative forecast is largely driven by a sharp worsening in risk disclosure tone and the introduction of a new supply-chain risk in the latest 10-K, relative to the firm's own history and sector peers."

This traceability not only helps with internal understanding and debugging, but is also essential for discussions with risk managers and compliance teams.

Validation Pitfalls Specific to Filings

Because filings are sparse and irregular in time, they create specific challenges for backtesting and validation.

Event sparsity and overfitting

For many firms, you only have a small number of years of high-quality filings. If you extract many features and then aggressively search for patterns, you risk fitting noise.

Mitigation strategies include:

- Pooling data across firms and sectors while controlling for industry effects.
- Using simple, robust features (e.g., coarse changes in tone) rather than overly granular metrics.

- Reserving out-of-sample periods and out-of-sample firms for validation.

Survivorship and look-ahead biases

It is easy to fall into the trap of building your filing dataset from firms that exist today. But some of the most interesting signals may come from firms that later delisted or went bankrupt.

To avoid survivorship bias:

- Construct the universe at each historical date using only firms that were actually listed then.
- Include delisted firms and their filings in the historical dataset.

As with all other signals, you must ensure that your backtests only use filings that would have been available by the decision time, with realistic lags.

Temptation of rare but spectacular disclosures

There is a natural temptation to build signals around memorable, rare events: fraud revelations, dramatic restatements, or crisis-era filings. While these cases provide good intuition, they are too sparse to support reliable statistical models on their own.

A disciplined approach is:

- Treat such spectacular events primarily as stress-test scenarios and qualitative case studies.
- Build core signals on more common, incremental changes in language and guidance.

Putting It All Together

By carefully reading long-form disclosures with LLMs, extracting structured and longitudinal features, and fusing them with traditional time-series predictors, we equip the autonomous analyst with a richer understanding of each firm's narrative and risk profile. These filing-based features tend to be:

- **Slower-moving** than news sentiment, reflecting deeper structural shifts.
- **Complementary** to numeric fundamentals and price-based signals.
- **Interpretable**, because each feature can be traced back to specific clauses and sections in the filings.

In the next section, we will take this expanded set of signals—from high-frequency news and events to slow-moving filing narratives—and connect them to portfolio construction and execution. There, we will show how forecasts informed by both text and numbers translate into positions, orders, and ultimately realized performance in the market.

6.3 Portfolio Construction, Execution, and Impact Modeling

In the previous sections we focused on building signals: turning heterogeneous text streams and long-form filings into structured forecasts of expected returns and risks. Those forecasts, however, are only potential energy. To turn them into realized performance, we must decide *how much* of each asset to hold, *how quickly* to trade, and *how to route orders* through real markets where transactions move prices.

This section explains how to connect text-informed alpha forecasts to implementable portfolios. We will:

- Formalize the forecasting output from the autonomous analyst: expected returns and uncertainties at the asset level.
- Introduce portfolio construction frameworks that translate forecasts into positions under risk budgets and constraints.
- Incorporate transaction-cost and market-impact models, so that trading frictions are considered at the design stage, not as an afterthought.
- Discuss execution tactics suited to sentiment and event-driven strategies, and how to learn from realized costs and slippage.

The outcome is an integrated loop: signals inform portfolios, portfolios generate trades, trades feed back realized costs and performance, and the entire system adapts.

From Text Signals to Alpha Forecasts

By now, the autonomous analyst can produce, for each asset i at time t:

- One or more **text-driven signals**: sentiment factors, event scores, filing-derived indicators.
- Traditional numeric features: valuation ratios, momentum indicators, risk-factor exposures.

A forecasting model combines these into an *expected excess return* (or alpha) $\hat{\mu}_{i,t}$ over a chosen horizon, such as one day or one month. In practice, we also care about:

- **Uncertainty or confidence**: a measure of how noisy or reliable the forecast is, which can depend on signal strength, model fit, and recent performance.
- **Signal source**: whether the alpha is coming from short-lived news sentiment, slow-moving filing language, or a mix.

For portfolio construction, it is helpful to organize the model output as:

- A vector of expected returns $\hat{\boldsymbol{\mu}}_t$ (one entry per asset).
- A risk model, such as a covariance matrix or factor model, that provides estimates of return variability and correlations.
- Optional: a per-asset forecast confidence or signal volatility measure, to tilt position sizes toward more reliable alphas.

With these ingredients, we can move from forecasts to weights.

Risk-Aware Portfolio Construction

Portfolio construction is the process of turning alpha forecasts into a set of target holdings that respect risk and practical constraints. We will keep the mathematics light and focus on intuition.

Core intuition: reward per unit of risk

Suppose you have two stocks, A and B. The model expects A to deliver 2% excess return next month and B to deliver 1%. If both have similar risk and are uncorrelated, you would naturally allocate more capital to A. If A is much riskier, you might scale back that tilt.

This "reward per unit of risk" idea generalizes. At a high level, a risk-aware portfolio optimizer tries to:

- Increase weights in assets with higher alpha forecasts.
- Decrease weights in assets with higher marginal contribution to portfolio risk.
- Respect constraints such as maximum leverage, concentration limits, and factor exposures.

Mean-variance optimization is one formalism that encodes this trade-off by balancing expected return against variance, but even simple heuristics (such as ranking alphas and capping position sizes) implicitly follow the same logic.

Incorporating forecast uncertainty

Not all alphas are created equal. For example:

- An alpha derived from a strong, consistent filing-based signal that has worked for years might be quite reliable.
- A spike in social-media sentiment around a small-cap stock might be noisy and fleeting.

You can reflect this by downweighting alphas with high uncertainty. A practical approach is:

- Estimate, for each signal or model, a historical error distribution.

- For each asset, compute an effective alpha that is reduced when forecast uncertainty is high.

Intuitively, you treat high-uncertainty forecasts as if they were "closer to zero" unless they are extremely strong.

Risk budgets and constraints

Real portfolios operate under multiple layers of constraints, many of which are particularly relevant for text-driven strategies:

- **Total risk budget**: cap expected volatility or value-at-risk so the portfolio remains within mandate.
- **Factor exposure limits**: constrain exposures to broad risk factors (market, size, value, sectors) so the portfolio's performance is not dominated by unintentional bets.
- **Concentration limits**: cap the weight in any single name or group, especially in less-liquid stocks where text signals may be strong but capacity is limited.
- **Turnover limits**: because sentiment- and news-driven signals can be very active, you may limit how much the portfolio can change from one rebalancing to the next to avoid excessive trading costs.
- **Regulatory and client-specific rules**: for example, no short positions in certain sectors, or minimum allocations to particular asset classes.

Mathematically, these show up as linear or nonlinear constraints in the optimizer. Conceptually, they limit how aggressively you can respond to text-driven alphas while keeping the overall risk profile controlled.

Adding Trading Costs and Market Impact

So far we have pretended that trading is free. In reality, *every* trade faces frictions:

- **Explicit costs**: commissions, fees, and taxes.

- **Bid–ask spread**: you typically buy at the offer and sell at the bid.
- **Slippage**: execution prices worse than mid-quote due to latency and competition.
- **Market impact**: your own orders move prices, especially in less-liquid names.

Text-driven strategies can be particularly exposed to these costs:

- News signals often demand fast reactions, when spreads are wide and liquidity is thin.
- Social-media-based signals may concentrate in small or crowded names.

Ignoring costs can turn an apparently attractive backtest into a losing live strategy. Instead, we build an explicit *transaction-cost model* and feed it into portfolio construction.

Stylized cost and impact models

A cost model maps a proposed trade size into an expected cost. A common structure decomposes costs into:

- A **fixed component**, such as half the bid–ask spread plus fees.
- A **variable component** that grows with trade size relative to market liquidity, often in a convex way (larger trades are disproportionately more expensive).

For example, you might specify that expected cost (in basis points) for trading a fraction q of average daily volume (ADV) is something like:

- a base cost (e.g., spread and fees), plus
- a term proportional to q, plus
- a term proportional to q^2.

The quadratic term captures market impact: doubling trade size more than doubles cost. While real models can be more sophisticated, this simple form already captures the key intuition: small trades in liquid names are cheap; large trades in illiquid names are expensive.

Linking costs to observable liquidity

To parameterize the cost model, you can tie it to observable quantities:

- Average daily dollar volume (ADV).
- Typical bid–ask spread.
- Recent volatility.
- Order book depth, if available.

For instance, impact coefficients might be higher in low-ADV, high-volatility stocks. Over time you will recalibrate these parameters by comparing predicted costs with realized execution outcomes.

Feeding costs back into the optimizer

Once you have a cost model, you can adjust portfolio construction in two main ways:

- **Cost-adjusted alphas**: subtract expected trading costs from raw alpha forecasts for each proposed trade. If the expected return from reacting to a sentiment signal is smaller than the cost of turning over the position, the trade is suppressed.
- **Explicit penalty in the objective**: include a term that penalizes turnover or cost, so the optimizer trades off extra return against extra cost.

The key idea is that the optimizer sees the net benefit of changing a position—expected incremental return minus expected incremental cost—and only executes trades when this net benefit is positive and meaningful.

Execution Tactics for Text-Driven Strategies

The portfolio optimizer outputs a set of *target positions*. The difference between current holdings and targets defines an *order list*: how many shares to buy or sell in each asset. Execution is the process of transforming that order list into actual trades in the market.

Text- and event-driven strategies pose special challenges for execution:

- Signals may decay quickly: a sentiment advantage after a news release might be strongest in the first few minutes or hours.
- Markets can be disrupted: around earnings or macro releases, spreads and volatility spike.

Execution tactics must balance urgency (trading quickly to capture alpha) against cost (trading slowly to reduce impact).

Urgency scheduling

A simple way to encode urgency is to decide what fraction of a target order to execute in each slice of time. Typical patterns include:

- **Front-loaded**: trade more aggressively early in the horizon. This is common for event-driven trades where early fills are more valuable.
- **Back-loaded**: trade more toward the end, perhaps when liquidity improves (for example, near the close for some markets).
- **Uniform or VWAP-like**: spread trading throughout the day in proportion to typical market volume patterns.

For a strong, fresh earnings surprise with a robust sentiment signal, you might choose a front-loaded schedule, accepting higher short-term costs to capture a rapidly decaying edge.

Slicing rules and participation constraints

Large parent orders are usually broken into many smaller *child orders* to hide their size and reduce impact. Common execution strategies include:

- **VWAP (Volume-Weighted Average Price)**: aim to match the market's volume profile over time.
- **POV (Percentage of Volume)**: participate in a fixed fraction of market volume at each instant (e.g., 10% of volume) so that you never dominate the tape.
- **Adaptive participation**: dynamically adjust participation based on real-time spreads, volatility, and market depth.

Text-driven strategies may need adaptive schemes. For example, right after a news shock, liquidity might be thin and volatility high; a prudent executor might briefly cap participation, then scale up as the order book refills and spreads normalize.

Safeguards: limits, throttles, and filters

To protect the strategy from pathological conditions and model errors, execution layers commonly enforce safeguards:

- **Limit prices**: cap the acceptable price for a buy or sell to avoid extreme prints in volatile conditions.
- **Volatility throttles**: slow or suspend trading when intraday volatility or spreads breach thresholds.
- **Liquidity filters**: avoid trading in names whose available liquidity has collapsed relative to normal (e.g., a stock under trading halt risk).

These mechanisms are especially important for autonomous systems that might otherwise respond too mechanically to text signals during crises or data glitches.

A Layered Architecture: From Signals to Execution

It is useful to visualize the full stack of components we have introduced: signals and forecasts at the top, portfolio construction in the middle, and execution at the bottom, with feedback loops running upward from realized costs and performance.

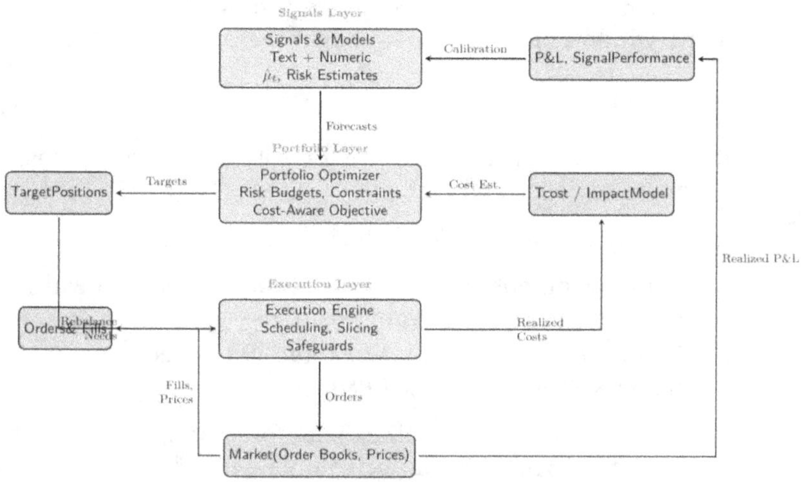

This diagram emphasizes that cost modeling and feedback are integral, not peripheral. The transaction-cost model informs the optimizer before trades are placed, and is itself updated using realized execution data.

Learning from Live Performance

Once the full system is in production, the autonomous analyst should continuously evaluate and adapt:

- **Signal diagnostics**: Is the incremental contribution of text-based features to forecast accuracy stable, improving, or degrading? This includes checking whether certain event types or sentiment categories still behave as they did in backtests.
- **Cost model calibration**: Do realized execution costs systematically exceed model predictions, especially around news and events? If so, adjust impact parameters or change execution tactics.
- **Regime detection**: Are there periods when text-driven signals invert (e.g., during crises when all news is bad but prices over-

react then mean-revert)? Simple regime-switching models or rolling-window analyses can highlight these shifts.

A practical workflow is:

- On each rebalancing cycle, record forecasts, target portfolios, realized trades, costs, and P&L.
- Periodically decompose P&L into:
  - *Signal component*: what you would have earned with frictionless trading given your positions.
  - *Timing and cost component*: the difference between frictionless P&L and realized P&L.
- Use this decomposition to adjust both forecasting models (if signals underperform) and trading components (if costs are higher than anticipated).

Putting It All Together

Text-informed alphas are powerful but fragile: they can be short-lived, noisy, and concentrated in challenging parts of the market. To harness them responsibly:

- Treat them as inputs to a disciplined, risk-aware portfolio construction process that respects constraints and risk budgets.
- Explicitly model transaction costs and market impact, and integrate those models into optimization rather than adjusting ex post.
- Use execution tactics—urgency scheduling, slicing, safeguards—that are tailored to the time sensitivity and liquidity profile of text-driven signals.
- Maintain a feedback loop from realized performance back to both the forecasting and execution layers.

Only when all three layers—signals, portfolios, and execution—work together coherently does the autonomous analyst deliver robust, repeatable value from LLM- and transformer-based market insight.

Chapter 7

Evaluation, Backtesting, and Operational Governance

Every profitable backtest can look like genius in hindsight. This chapter is about making sure your autonomous analyst survives contact with the live market. We move from leakage-proof evaluation and honest walk-forward testing, through risk-aware and causally grounded research, to the operational guardrails-monitoring, governance, and compliance-that keep LLM-driven systems both profitable and permissible in production.

7.1 Leakage Control, Benchmarks, and Backtesting Discipline

In the previous chapter we treated LLMs as powerful but opinionated analysts: they read disclosures, news, and market context, then emit structured views that can be turned into trades. This section asks a harder question: *how do we know those trades would still work once we leave the notebook and step into the market?*

For LLM-driven strategies, optimism in backtests is cheap and abundant. What is scarce is *reliable* evidence that the signal survives realistic data flows, execution costs, and model updates. Three ideas dominate this reliability problem:

- controlling data leakage so the model never "peeks" at the future;
- designing benchmarks that an LLM must beat to justify its complexity; and
- enforcing disciplined, walk-forward backtesting procedures that mirror live deployment.

We will build these ideas step by step, always tying abstract evaluation choices back to the concrete realities of time, information arrival, and trading frictions.

A Taxonomy of Leakage in LLM-Based Trading

Why leakage is especially dangerous with LLMs

Data leakage means that information from the future, or from the target label, slips into the model's inputs or training process. Any such leak makes the backtest look too good. In traditional factor models, leakage might come from using a revised macro series that was not yet published at trade time. In LLM systems the surface area for leakage is much larger:

- LLMs consume rich context: news, filings, social media, broker research, embeddings, and retrieval results.
- They are often fine-tuned or prompt-tuned on historical examples that are not cleanly separated from evaluation data.
- Pretraining corpora frequently contain exactly the texts you later use for evaluation.

Unless time and information sets are handled with care, an LLM can exploit details that were unknowable to any real trader at that moment.

Temporal leakage: when the clock runs backwards

Temporal leakage occurs whenever an input includes information that was not yet available at the decision time. Common paths:

- Using end-of-day prices or volume to label and also to construct features that are timestamped earlier in the day.
- Feeding quarterly filings or earnings call transcripts into prompts dated *before* those documents were released.
- Creating embeddings or document retrieval indexes from a full-history corpus, then using them to answer "as of 2016" questions that can silently retrieve a 2019 article.

The intuitive test is: *could a trader in that moment, with that data feed, have known this piece of information?* If the answer is no, you have temporal leakage.

LLM workflows introduce two additional twists:

- **Pretraining leakage.** If the base model was pretrained on news and filings up to a given year, then at evaluation time it may "remember" specific events or outcomes, even if you do not explicitly include them in the prompt. For example, asking "What is your outlook for Company X on January 15, 2018?" may elicit an answer that is implicitly conditioned on knowledge of what happened later that year.
- **Retrieval leakage.** Retrieval-augmented generation (RAG) pipelines often build a single global index over text. If you then query this index for historical dates, you must ensure that the retrieval engine only sees documents with timestamps prior to the decision date. Otherwise, seemingly harmless retrieval calls leak the future.

Cross-asset and cross-entity leakage

Markets are entangled. A leak in one instrument can become a leak in another.

- **Index versus constituents.** Suppose you train on S&P 500 index returns and then test on an individual constituent. If the index return at time t is used as a feature and you forecast the stock's return at the same horizon, you may be using a feature whose path is partially determined by that very stock.

- **Corporate families and ADRs.** Related entities (parent, subsidiary, ADR, dual listings) can reveal each other's future through highly correlated news and price reactions. If your train and test splits separate by ticker but not by economic group, you may overstate generalization.

- **Embedding confusion.** If you build dense embeddings of securities or issuers using full-history text, similar entities can pull each other's future information into their representation, especially when you subsequently keep embeddings fixed over all time.

The remedy is to think not just in terms of "rows" in a dataset, but in terms of economic *clusters*. Splits should, where possible, separate clusters, not just individual securities.

Label leakage via text and preprocessing

Label leakage happens when labels (e.g., future returns, earnings surprises) are directly or indirectly encoded in the text that the model sees.

Examples that occur frequently in LLM research:

- Using news articles that summarize an event *after* the market has reacted ("Shares of Company X jumped 15% today after beating earnings estimates...") as if they were the text available *before* the price move.

- Generating training prompts from historical data where you include the label or a trivial transformation of it in the context ("The stock went up 5% in the next week. Explain why.") and then reusing those texts or embeddings in other tasks.

- Including derived signals (e.g., analyst "buy" or "sell" flags that themselves were built from the target returns) alongside raw text in the same input without clear lineage.

In practice, any preprocessing step that joins text, prices, and labels must be audited: which fields are computed using information beyond the decision time? Are those fields ever passed, even indirectly, into the LLM as input or into the selection of training examples?

Designing Leakage-Resistant Data Pipelines

Event-time indexing and feature windows

To control leakage, anchor everything to *event time*. For each decision or forecast you want to evaluate:

- Define a decision timestamp t (e.g., 15:55 New York time for same-day close orders, or 08:00 for pre-market decisions).
- Construct features using only data with timestamps $\leq t$.
- Define a prediction horizon (e.g., next-day close to close), and compute labels using only data in $(t, t + \Delta]$.

For LLM-based signals, this means:

- Associate each document (news article, filing, tweet, transcript snippet) with the time it first became available to your hypothetical trading system.
- When forming a prompt for time t, include only documents with publication time strictly before t.
- When using embeddings or RAG, build time-bounded indexes (e.g., monthly or quarterly) so that any retrieval call at time t searches only documents with timestamps $\leq t$.

Feature windows (e.g., "last 30 days of news sentiment") should be implemented by explicit filters on timestamp rather than by joining on calendar dates alone.

Embargo periods and lookahead buffers

Financial data can be messy around event times. Prices may reflect leaked information before an official announcement; corporate actions may be backdated; news feeds can have slight delivery lags. To be conservative, practitioners often use *embargo periods* and *lookahead buffers*:

- An **embargo period** is a gap between the end of a training window and the start of the test window. Data in the embargo is not used for training or evaluation. It reduces the risk that overlapping positions or slow information diffusion cause subtle leakage between adjacent windows.
- A **lookahead buffer** shrinks the feature window to end at $t - \epsilon$, where ϵ is a small time margin (e.g., 5 minutes or 1 bar) before the decision time. This accounts for delays in data feeds or text availability.

In LLM workflows, embargoes are useful when your prompts explicitly reference prior model forecasts or "rationales," which could otherwise bleed across windows, and when your RAG index is updated in batches.

Sanitizing text and prompts

To prevent label leakage via text:

- Exclude obviously post-hoc documents (e.g., "recap" news that is timestamped after the price move you are trying to predict).
- When in doubt, tag each document with a field indicating whether it is *preview* (before the event), *concurrent*, or *summary* (after the event), and restrict prompts to the first two.
- Avoid prompt templates that include ex-post performance in the context. If you are training an explanation model ("Why did the stock move?"), keep that dataset entirely separate from the predictive backtesting pipeline.

A useful habit is to log, for every backtest example, all document IDs and timestamps actually presented to the LLM. Periodic random audits of these logs often reveal overlooked leaks.

Temporal Splits and Walk-Forward Evaluation

Once the dataset is leak-resistant at the row level, the next step is to structure the *time splits* between training, validation, and test.

From random splits to temporal splits

Randomly shuffling rows into train and test sets is standard in many machine learning domains, but in finance it creates unrealistic optimism. The future frequently looks different from the past: volatility regimes shift, sector composition changes, and new types of events appear.

For time-series and panel data, you want *temporal splits*:

- **Training window:** a contiguous block of historical time used for fitting the model or calibrating prompts.
- **Validation window:** the subsequent block used for model selection and hyperparameter tuning.
- **Test window:** a final, untouched block representing truly out-of-sample performance.

The ordering must respect calendar time: all training data come before validation, which in turn comes before test.

Walk-forward and expanding windows

In production you do not train once and run forever. Models and prompts are periodically refreshed as new data arrive. Walk-forward evaluation mimics this:

- Pick an initial training window (e.g., 2012–2016), a validation window (2017), and a test window (2018).

- Train and tune the model using 2012–2017, then evaluate on 2018.
- Roll the windows forward by some step (e.g., one year), retrain and retune using all data up to the new cutoff, and test on the next period.

Two common patterns:

- **Expanding window:** training data grow over time (2012–2016, then 2012–2017, then 2012–2018, and so on). This matches workflows where you keep accumulating more history.
- **Rolling window:** the training window has fixed length (e.g., most recent 5 years) and slides through time. This is useful when very old data are believed to be less relevant.

For LLMs, walk-forward evaluation encompasses not just refitting numerical models, but also:

- updating retrieval indexes and embeddings only with data up to the current cutoff;
- re-tuning prompts or few-shot exemplars using only historical examples; and
- possibly changing the LLM itself (e.g., moving from one model version to another) according to rules frozen before seeing the next test window.

Visualizing temporal splits and leakage points

The logic of temporal splits and leakage is easier to grasp with a timeline.

This figure highlights three ideas: contiguous train/validation/test blocks, walk-forward shifts over time, and specific "hot spots" where future text or labels often sneak into features or prompts.

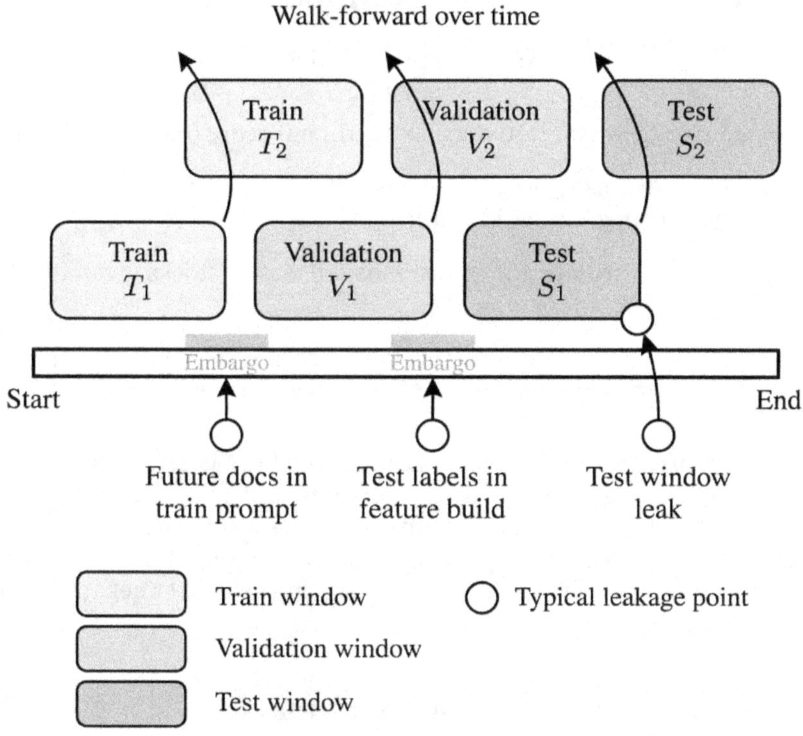
Walk-forward over time
Train
T_2
Validation
V_2
Test
S_2
Train
T_1
Validation
V_1
Test
S_1
Embargo
Embargo
Start
End
Future docs in train prompt
Test labels in feature build
Test window leak
Train window
Validation window
Test window
Typical leakage point

From Language Outputs to Trading Benchmarks

Once you trust the temporal structure, you must ask: *compared to what?* A backtest Sharpe ratio of 1.0 is meaningless unless you know the baseline performance of simpler alternatives on the same data and constraints.

Defining what the LLM is supposed to improve

LLMs can play several roles in a trading pipeline:

- convert raw text into a scalar sentiment score (e.g., bullishness);
- produce categorical views (e.g., upgrade/downgrade, positive/negative guidance);
- rank securities (e.g., "top 10 most attractive stocks given today's news"); or
- generate richer outputs (rationales, scenario narratives) that are then post-processed into actions.

Your benchmark must match this role. If the LLM is generating a daily cross-sectional ranking, a natural benchmark is a simple ranking rule built from conventional text sentiment or price momentum. If the LLM outputs "buy/hold/sell" signals, the benchmark might be a naive rule that buys after positive earnings surprises and sells after negative ones, with no text at all.

Naïve and factor-based benchmarks

A robust evaluation stack typically includes at least three layers of benchmarks:

- **Naïve heuristics.** Examples: buy-and-hold the universe; sector-neutral equal-weighted portfolio; simple price trend-following. These tell you whether the LLM adds anything beyond what any intern could implement in an afternoon.

- **Classical factor models.** Use well-known factors (value, momentum, quality, size, low volatility) as either explanatory variables or as alternative alpha signals. Your LLM strategy should be compared to portfolios that tilt on those factors, under the same leverage and turnover constraints.
- **Text-only baselines.** Use off-the-shelf bag-of-words, TF-IDF, or simple lexicon sentiment models on the same text corpus. This isolates the incremental value of a large language model over traditional NLP.

The goal is not to embarrass the LLM; it is to avoid fooling yourself. If a bag-of-words sentiment model delivers similar risk-adjusted returns with lower complexity and cost, it deserves serious consideration.

Task-level metrics linked to P&L

While portfolio-level metrics (Sharpe ratio, maximum drawdown, turnover, hit rate) are ultimately what matters, it is helpful to measure the *intermediate* quality of the LLM's outputs.

Common task-level metrics include:

- **Directional accuracy:** fraction of times the sign of the LLM-implied return (up or down) matches the realized return over the prediction horizon.
- **Calibration:** if the model says "70% chance of positive return," does the event actually occur about 70% of the time over many such predictions?
- **Ranking metrics:** precision@K or information coefficient (rank correlation) between the LLM's ranking and realized returns, especially useful in long-short or relative-value strategies.
- **Cost-aware utility scores:** simple scoring rules that subtract estimated transaction costs and capacity limits to approximate net contribution to P&L.

These metrics link language performance to trading relevance. For instance, an LLM that writes beautiful narratives but has poor ranking correlation with returns is a good research assistant, but a weak signal generator.

Pragmatic Backtesting Discipline

Finally, we integrate leakage control and benchmarks into a disciplined backtesting protocol.

Clear in-sample, validation, and out-of-sample periods

A minimal discipline has three chronological regions:

- **In-sample (training).** Used to fit any learnable components: numerical models, prompt templates, or calibration layers that map LLM scores to trading positions.
- **Validation.** Used to decide among alternative prompts, hyperparameters, position-sizing rules, and cost assumptions. Any choice you make while looking at performance numbers is, by definition, tuned on the validation period.
- **Out-of-sample (test).** Kept invisible until the very end. Used once to estimate performance, to be shown to a risk committee or investment board. If you iterate on the model after seeing test results, that data ceases to be true out-of-sample; you must either move the test window forward or treat it as part of validation.

For LLMs, "hyperparameters" include not just numeric values, but prompt wording, context window choices, retrieval depth, and aggregation rules. You should treat prompt redesign after seeing validation results as tuning, and avoid using test windows in that loop.

Execution modeling and slippage

Realistic backtests include frictions:

- **Transaction costs:** explicit commissions, bid-ask spreads, and estimated market impact as a function of turnover and volume.
- **Slippage:** deviation between model's reference price (often close or mid) and actual execution price. This can be modeled as a function of liquidity and order size.
- **Timing constraints:** if the LLM needs minutes to read and score a long filing, assume that orders are executed later in the session, not at the instant of event timestamp.

In LLM stacks there is also the question of **inference latency**. If prompt processing and retrieval take, say, several seconds per security, you must either:

- restrict the number of securities scored in real time;
- precompute scores in batch (e.g., overnight) and adjust the strategy definition accordingly; or
- accept that some fast intraday reactions are out of reach.

Your backtest should adopt exactly the timing and latency assumptions you can support in production.

Nested cross-validation for model and prompt selection

When you have many candidate prompts, retrieval settings, or post-processing rules, overfitting to the validation window is a real risk. *Nested* cross-validation mitigates this:

- Split the historical period into multiple folds of train/validation/test, each respecting temporal order.
- For each fold, use the inner train/validation portions to select prompts and hyperparameters.
- Evaluate the chosen configuration on that fold's test window.

Aggregating performance across folds yields a more stable estimate of how often your selection process would have picked a genuinely good configuration rather than merely one that flattered the specific validation interval.

Live-paper and shadow trading

Even after rigorous historical testing, LLM-based strategies should pass through a *paper-trading* phase before real capital is at risk:

- **Live-paper trading** runs the full production pipeline, including data ingestion, LLM calls, and order generation, but records hypothetical trades only in a sandbox. It exposes operational issues—latency spikes, missing data, model timeouts—that backtests cannot see.
- **Shadow trading** parallels an existing production strategy: the LLM-derived recommendations are compared in real time to actual trades, but do not influence them. This shows how the new signal behaves under current market conditions and capacity.

You should treat the live-paper phase as an additional out-of-sample test: resist the urge to "fix" the model too frequently based on early noise; instead, predefine performance and stability thresholds that, if met, justify moving to small-scale live deployment.

A readiness checklist for risk review

Before you present an LLM-driven strategy to a risk committee, you should be able to answer, with evidence:

- **Leakage:** How do you ensure that no future text, prices, or labels enter the inputs or training of the strategy? Can you show an audit trail for a random day?
- **Temporal splits:** How were training, validation, and test windows chosen? How many independent test windows have you evaluated, and how stable are the results across them?

- **Benchmarks:** Which naive and factor-based benchmarks did you use? How much incremental risk-adjusted return does the LLM provide after costs?
- **Backtesting realism:** What execution costs, slippage, and latency assumptions did you adopt? Are these anchored in actual trading experience or external data?
- **Robustness:** How sensitive are results to reasonable variations in prompts, retrieval settings, and position-sizing rules?

A strategy that cannot answer these questions is not ready, no matter how attractive the Sharpe ratio looks in the notebook. Conversely, a well-documented, leakage-resistant, benchmark-aware, and walk-forward tested LLM strategy has a genuine chance of surviving first contact with live markets.

7.2 Risk Management, Causal Inference, and Multiple Testing

In the previous section we focused on *whether* an LLM-driven strategy appears to work out of sample: we fought data leakage, designed realistic walk-forward tests, and compared LLMs to simple benchmarks. In this section we shift from "Does it work?" to "*What kind of risk are we taking, why does it work, and how likely is it that we just got lucky?*"

Three themes structure the discussion:

- connecting model performance to portfolio-level risk and capital usage;
- using causal reasoning to distinguish genuine edges from artifacts; and
- controlling false discoveries when you test many models, prompts, and signals.

Throughout, you should keep one picture in mind: an LLM signal does not live in isolation. It sits inside a portfolio, in a changing market environment, and inside a research process that may generate thousands of candidate ideas. Risk management, causal inference, and multiple-testing discipline are safeguards at each of these three layers.

From Forecast Errors to Portfolio Risk

Why raw accuracy is not enough

Backtests often start and end with a small set of statistics: hit rate, mean absolute error, or Sharpe ratio. While these are useful, they say little about *where* risk comes from or how errors translate into drawdowns.

For instance:

- A model with moderate accuracy but very aggressive position sizing can generate severe drawdowns.
- A model that is accurate in calm periods but fails in crises may look fine in a long backtest, yet be unacceptable for a risk-averse investor.
- A model that is modestly profitable but highly correlated with existing books may add little diversification benefit.

To judge an LLM-based strategy properly, you must move from signal-level metrics to *risk-aware* evaluation.

Mapping signal quality to portfolio outcomes

Consider a simple setup: each day the LLM assigns a score to each stock (e.g., predicted next-week return), and a downstream layer converts these scores into positions. Noise in the scores leads to three main portfolio effects:

- **Volatility and drawdown.** If score errors are large and uncorrelated across names, they add to idiosyncratic risk. If they are systematically wrong in specific regimes (e.g., highly optimistic in bear markets), they create *state-dependent* drawdowns.

- **Turnover and trading cost.** If scores fluctuate noisily, the portfolio rebalances frequently, increasing turnover and costs. A slightly more accurate but much more unstable signal may be worse after costs than a simpler, smoother benchmark.
- **Tail risk.** Occasional extreme mispredictions can generate concentrated bets in the wrong direction, especially if the position-sizing rule extrapolates aggressively from high scores.

A practical way to connect evaluation to risk is to track, alongside each backtest:

- distribution of position sizes as a function of score;
- realized turnover, both gross and net;
- drawdown statistics (maximum, average over rolling windows);
- exposure to standard risk factors (market, sectors, styles); and
- marginal contribution to portfolio volatility from the LLM-driven sleeve.

These quantities are easy to compute from simulated trades and returns. They translate "an LLM with 55% hit rate" into "a strategy that adds 10% annualized volatility and a historical worst drawdown of 20%".

Scenario and stress testing for text-driven strategies

LLM signals are often most active exactly when markets are stressful: during news shocks, regime changes, or high-volatility events. You should therefore ask:

- How did the strategy behave around major macro events (elections, rate decisions, crises)?
- How does it handle periods with surges in news volume about a few names or sectors?

- Does the LLM remain calibrated when the overall tone of news shifts rapidly (e.g., during sudden policy announcements)?

Stress testing can be done in two complementary ways:

Historical scenarios. Isolate time windows around known events and study the strategy's realized returns, turnover, and exposures. This identifies specific vulnerabilities (e.g., the model systematically buys into negative earnings surprises because it misreads cautious language).

Hypothetical scenarios. Create synthetic shocks to inputs or parameters: for example, scale down all positive news sentiment scores by 50%, delay all text by one day, or cap maximum position sizes. Observe how P&L and drawdowns change. Such experiments reveal how dependent the strategy is on precise LLM outputs and timing assumptions.

Stress testing should be integrated into your evaluation pipeline, not treated as an afterthought. For LLM systems, the goal is to ensure that small model misinterpretations do not turn into large portfolio accidents in turbulent periods.

Explainability and prompt sensitivity

Because LLMs are complex and non-linear, you want tools that link their text-based reasoning to risk:

- **Token or phrase attributions.** For a given document and prediction, highlight which words or phrases contributed most to the model's score. If you see spurious cues (e.g., overreacting to generic legal boilerplate), this signals fragility.
- **Prompt sensitivity analysis.** Perturb the prompt wording or ordering of context documents and measure changes in predictions. Excessive sensitivity suggests that any live change to templates could alter the risk profile materially.
- **Marginal risk contribution per feature.** For hybrid models that combine text-derived features with numerical ones, compute how much each feature (or family of features) contributes

to portfolio variance and drawdown. This can be approximated by re-running backtests with that feature disabled.

These tools help you answer questions from risk managers such as: "What kinds of text does the model respond to? Are these stable over time? Is the strategy relying heavily on one fragile pattern in language or on a diversified set of cues?"

Causal Inference: Is the Edge Real or an Illusion?

So far we have treated the LLM's predictive power as a black box: if it forecasts returns, we trade. But markets are full of correlations that appear predictive in historical data yet vanish in live trading. Causal reasoning provides a lens to separate mere association from plausible cause-and-effect.

Treatments, outcomes, and confounders in markets

In causal inference, a *treatment* is an action or condition whose effect you care about, and an *outcome* is what you measure. In trading, examples include:

- Treatment: "firm issues unusually positive guidance language"; outcome: "subsequent 5-day stock return."
- Treatment: "portfolio uses LLM-enhanced routing for order execution"; outcome: "average trading cost per share."
- Treatment: "investor reads an LLM-generated news summary that highlights certain risks"; outcome: "change in position size."

A *confounder* is a variable that influences both treatment and outcome. For example, firm quality might drive both upbeat language *and* strong returns. If you do not control for quality, you may overstate the effect of language itself.

In LLM-based strategies, confounders are everywhere:

- firm size and liquidity;

- coverage by analysts and media (popular names get more text);
- sector membership and macro sensitivity;
- existing factor exposures in your portfolio.

Causal inference asks: if we adjust for these confounders, does the apparent predictive power of the LLM signal persist?

Event studies for text signals

An event study is a simple but powerful design that fits naturally with text-driven signals. The idea is:

- Identify an event date (e.g., earnings announcement, major news release).
- Define an event window around it (e.g., $[-1, +3]$ trading days).
- Measure abnormal returns in this window relative to a benchmark model (e.g., market model, factor model).
- Compare abnormal returns across groups defined by the LLM's assessment of the event (e.g., "strongly positive tone" vs. "strongly negative tone").

If, after controlling for market and factor exposures, the "strongly positive" group systematically outperforms the "strongly negative" group, you have evidence that the LLM's interpretation of the event is capturing something beyond standard factors.

Two important cautions:

- Ensure that the LLM only sees text available before or at the event time (avoid post-event summaries).
- Stratify or control for confounders such as firm size and prior momentum when grouping events.

Event studies help translate a fuzzy statement ("the LLM seems to understand guidance tone") into a quantitative claim ("conditional on sector, size, and factors, positive-tone events exhibit on average 1.2% higher 3-day abnormal returns").

Difference-in-differences in trading interventions

Sometimes the LLM changes a *process* rather than a prediction. For example, you may adopt LLM-based pre-trade analysis for a subset of instruments or desks. Here, a *difference-in-differences* (DiD) design can be useful.

The basic recipe:

- Define a treatment group (e.g., desks that start using the LLM tool) and a control group (similar desks that do not).
- Measure the outcome (e.g., implementation shortfall, risk-adjusted returns) before and after the LLM adoption for both groups.
- Compute the difference in the change: (treated after - treated before) minus (control after - control before).

If this "difference-in-differences" is significantly positive, and the groups are otherwise comparable, you have evidence that the LLM tool caused an improvement, rather than coinciding with broader favorable conditions.

The DiD logic can also be applied synthetically within backtests, for instance by simulating adoption of the LLM signal only for certain sectors or time periods while holding others fixed as a control.

Instrumental variables and selection bias

In real markets, your strategy may only be applied when conditions look favorable. For example, portfolio managers might choose to follow the LLM's recommendation only for highly liquid stocks or when its confidence score is high. This creates *selection bias*: performance conditional on "chosen" trades overstates the effect of the LLM itself.

Instrumental variable (IV) strategies offer one possible remedy. An *instrument* is a variable that:

- affects whether the LLM recommendation is acted upon (treatment); but

- does not directly affect the outcome except through that treatment.

In practice, credible instruments are difficult to find, but occasionally you can leverage quasi-random variation: workload differences across desks, staggered rollout schedules, or exogenous outages of the LLM service. When present, such variation helps you estimate how much of the observed performance truly stems from the LLM, as opposed to manager discretion.

Even when formal IV methods are not feasible, merely asking "What factors determine when we use the LLM's output? How might those also influence returns?" helps you design fairer evaluations.

Multiple Testing and the Research Factory Problem

Modern LLM workflows make it easy to generate thousands of variants: different prompts, context windows, scoring rules, and portfolio constructions. If you test enough ideas on the same historical data, you are *guaranteed* to find some that look great by pure chance. This is the multiple-testing problem.

How false discoveries explode

Imagine that you evaluate 1,000 unrelated strategies on a dataset where none has true predictive power. If your decision rule is "deploy anything with a 5% significance level" or "any backtest Sharpe above 1," you will, on average, flag around 50 strategies as "significant" purely by luck.

This is the core issue:

- The more tests you run on the same data, the higher the probability of false positives.
- LLMs, with flexible prompting and rich feature sets, enlarge the space of possible tests dramatically.

Naively picking the best-looking backtest from a large search is equivalent to cherry-picking noise. To keep the research process honest, you need explicit multiple-testing controls.

Family-wise error rate vs. false discovery rate

Two related concepts guide correction methods:

Family-wise error rate (FWER). The probability of making *at least one* false discovery in a family of tests. Controlling FWER is strict: it aims to make false positives rare, but may be conservative (you miss some true signals).

False discovery rate (FDR). The expected proportion of false discoveries among all discoveries you declare. Controlling FDR accepts that some selected strategies may be false positives, but keeps their fraction under control.

In a trading research factory where you expect some real signals but also a lot of noise, FDR control is often more practical: you are willing to investigate a basket of candidates as long as the majority are likely genuine.

Bonferroni and related corrections

The simplest FWER control is the Bonferroni correction:

- If you run m tests and want the overall chance of any false positive to be at most α (e.g., 5%), require each individual test to meet a significance level of α/m.

For example, if $m = 100$, you would demand p-values below 0.0005 for each strategy, or equivalently, much higher t-statistics than usual. This greatly reduces false positives, but also discards many potentially useful signals when m is large.

There are more refined FWER controls (e.g., Holm's method) that are slightly less conservative, but the key idea is the same: significance thresholds must be tightened when many tests are run.

Benjamini-Hochberg false discovery rate control

The Benjamini-Hochberg (BH) procedure is widely used to control FDR:

- Compute p-values for all m tested strategies.
- Sort them from smallest to largest: $p_{(1)} \le p_{(2)} \le \cdots \le p_{(m)}$.
- For a desired FDR level q (e.g., 10%), find the largest index k such that
$$p_{(k)} \le \frac{k}{m} q.$$
- Declare the first k strategies (those with the smallest p-values) as discoveries.

Intuitively, BH allows more discoveries when many tests have low p-values (suggesting real signal) and fewer when the distribution of p-values looks mostly uniform (suggesting noise). It adjusts to the strength of evidence in the entire family rather than applying a blanket Bonferroni cutoff.

In the LLM context, you can treat each distinct combination of prompt, retrieval settings, and post-processing rule as a "strategy" in the BH procedure.

Holdout discovery sets and staggered validation

Statistical corrections are powerful, but they rely on assumptions about independence and distribution of tests that may not fully hold in finance. A complementary, more intuitive tool is the *holdout discovery set.*

The idea:

- Partition your historical data into three chronological pieces: development, discovery, and confirmation.
- Use the **development** period to freely explore models, prompts, and ideas, without making binding decisions.

- On the **discovery** period, formally test a curated set of promising strategies, applying multiple-testing corrections (FWER/FDR) to decide which are worthy of deeper study.
- Reserve the **confirmation** period as a final, untouched out-of-sample window to evaluate only the small set of strategies that passed discovery.

This staggered approach has two benefits:

- It acknowledges and quarantines the messy, exploratory phase of LLM research.
- It keeps a portion of data completely shielded from the bulk of testing so that final performance estimates are less contaminated by data mining.

In practice, your research culture should reflect this structure: exploratory notebooks are welcomed, but only strategies that survive formal discovery and confirmation phases reach risk committees.

An Integrated View: Go/No-Go for Production

Risk management, causal inference, and multiple-testing control are not separate boxes to tick. Together with the leakage and backtesting discipline from the previous section, they form a unified gatekeeping framework that turns backtest optimism into a sober go/no-go decision.

Before green-lighting an LLM-based strategy, you should be able to articulate:

- **Risk profile.** What are the main sources of volatility, drawdowns, and tail risk? How do these behave across scenarios, especially in crises or during news surges?
- **Mechanism.** Why should this signal exist? Is there a plausible narrative linking the LLM's interpretation of text to subsequent returns, surviving basic causal scrutiny (event studies, controls for confounders)?

- **Discovery discipline.** Out of how many tried variants did this model emerge? What multiple-testing adjustments were applied, and on which data splits?
- **Robustness.** Does the signal persist, with similar sign and magnitude, when you vary reasonable modeling choices (alternative prompts, slightly different horizons, conservative cost assumptions)?

If you cannot answer these questions with concrete analyses, the correct decision is to continue research rather than deploy. The point is not to eliminate all uncertainty-that is impossible in markets-but to ensure that any remaining uncertainty is clearly understood, proportionate to the expected reward, and acceptable within the firm's risk appetite.

In the next section we will move from research to operations: how to serve LLMs in production, monitor them over time, and embed them within governance frameworks that satisfy both internal and regulatory standards.

7.3 Serving, Monitoring, and Compliance in Production

Up to this point, we have treated LLMs as research instruments. We carefully avoided leakage, compared them to benchmarks, and examined their risk and statistical credibility. In practice, however, no investor is paid for backtests. Value is created when a vetted signal is woven into a live trading system that is fast, reliable, monitored, and governable.

This section explains how to make that transition. We will:

- outline architectural patterns for serving LLMs in latency-sensitive trading contexts;
- describe monitoring and guardrails that track both technical health and financial performance; and

- connect LLM stacks to model risk management and regulatory expectations around documentation, controls, and auditability.

The goal is to make the "autonomous analyst" not just smart, but also safe and accountable.

From Research Notebook to Production Stack

In research, you can tolerate occasional timeouts, manual restarts, or ad hoc data fixes. In production, every component must behave predictably under load and failure. The first step is to crystallize the high-level architecture of your LLM-based trading system.

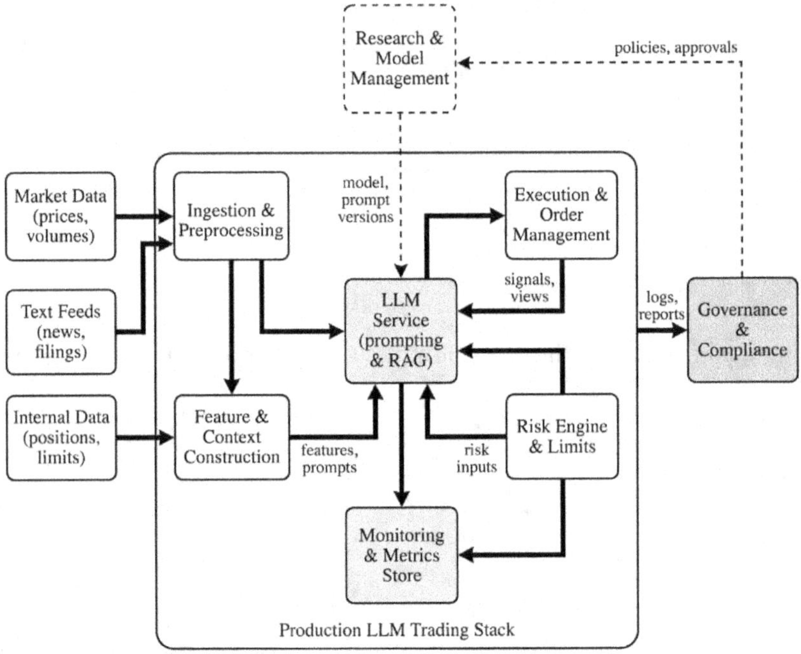

This diagram emphasizes three separations:

- between *data sources* and *preprocessing*;
- between the *LLM service* and downstream trading and risk components; and
- between the *production stack* and the surrounding governance and research processes.

Keeping these layers distinct simplifies reasoning about failures and responsibilities: a data glitch is not a model bug; a model drift is not a limit-engine defect.

Serving Architectures: Real-Time vs. Batch

Clarifying latency requirements

Before choosing any specific serving architecture, you must answer a practical question: *How fast does the LLM need to respond for this use case to be valuable?*

Common categories include:

- **Intraday, latency-sensitive.** For example, reacting to breaking news within seconds or minutes to trade before the bulk of the market.
- **End-of-day or overnight.** For example, generating daily cross-sectional rankings or updating risk scenarios based on the day's disclosures.
- **Human-in-the-loop research.** For example, assisting analysts with summaries; here, seconds of latency are typically fine.

In general, the more time-sensitive the use case, the stronger the constraints on model size, context length, and number of securities processed.

Real-time inference patterns

For real-time strategies, you typically adopt a service-oriented architecture:

- The LLM runs behind a low-latency API, horizontally scalable across multiple instances.
- A thin *orchestration layer* handles prompt construction, retrieval queries, and response parsing.
- A request may be triggered by events (e.g., "new headline on stock X") or by a fixed schedule (e.g., every five minutes).

To meet strict response-time targets, you may need:

- **Caching.** Cache embeddings, retrieved document sets, and even full LLM responses for frequently asked contexts (e.g., stable company descriptions) to avoid recomputation.
- **Prompt templates as configuration.** Treat prompts as versioned configuration objects, not inline code strings, so that changes can be tested and rolled out without redeploying services.
- **Model routing.** Use smaller, faster models for routine tasks (such as sentiment classification) and reserve larger, slower models for complex edge cases. A simple router can decide which model to call based on input type or confidence thresholds.

Every millisecond counts in such setups, so you often have to trade off model richness against throughput and cost.

Batch and hybrid processing

Many valuable uses of LLMs in trading do not demand millisecond responses. For example:

- scoring all companies' annual reports once a year;
- summarizing and classifying earnings transcripts overnight; or
- producing daily "heat maps" of news sentiment by sector.

These are well suited to *batch processing*:

- Jobs are scheduled (e.g., nightly or weekly) and run on scalable compute clusters.
- Results are stored in a feature store and used by downstream models or reports without direct calls to the LLM during trading hours.

A *hybrid* design is also common: bulk scoring and summarization in batch, combined with selectively triggered real-time calls for genuinely surprising events. This helps keep operational risk and inference costs under control.

Reliability and Graceful Degradation

Serving an LLM in production means accepting that things will go wrong: upstream feeds may go down, the model service may experience latency spikes, or a new version may misbehave. A robust system is judged not by the absence of failures, but by how safely it behaves *when* failures occur.

Service-level objectives

It is good practice to define explicit service-level objectives (SLOs) for the LLM component, such as:

- 99% of responses under 500 milliseconds for specific request types;
- 99.5% availability during trading hours;
- upper bounds on average cost per request.

SLOs provide quantitative targets for capacity planning and set expectations for traders and risk managers. If the system cannot meet a required SLO, you must either simplify the use case or shift it to batch processing.

Fallbacks and safe defaults

Graceful degradation means defining what the system does *when the LLM is unavailable or slow.* For each downstream consumer you should agree on:

- **Fallback behaviors.** Examples: revert to a simpler baseline signal; freeze positions; or skip trades driven uniquely by the LLM.
- **Timeout policies.** For real-time calls, after a fixed timeout, the request should return a clear failure state and the downstream component should act accordingly.
- **Version rollback.** If a new LLM version or prompt template causes anomalies, you need a tested, one-click rollback path to the last known good configuration.

Importantly, these behaviors are risk decisions, not just engineering decisions. A risk committee should be comfortable with what happens to the portfolio when the AI component is degraded.

Resilience to bad inputs

News and market data are noisy and adversarial in a broad sense: typos, sarcasm, rumors, and even deliberate manipulation affect what the LLM sees. To reduce the impact of pathological inputs:

- Perform **input validation** and basic sanity checks before prompts are constructed (e.g., discard obviously malformed documents, cap document length, flag unusual language).
- Limit the effect of any single document or request on final positions. For instance, clip the maximum position change that can be attributed to a single newly ingested text.
- Maintain a blacklist or quarantine mechanism for sources known to be unreliable or prone to manipulation.

These controls complement the risk tools from earlier sections and are particularly important for text-heavy LLM use cases.

Monitoring: Technical, Statistical, and Business-Level

Once the system is live, continuous monitoring is the only way to detect drift, degradation, or outright failure before they become costly.

Technical health

Technical monitoring focuses on the mechanics of the LLM service:

- request rates, queue lengths, and response latencies;
- error rates (timeouts, malformed responses, upstream data failures);
- resource utilization (CPU, GPU, memory) and cost per request.

Standard observability tools (metrics, logs, distributed tracing) apply here, but they should be tied to trading calendars and critical windows: a 2-second latency spike at midnight is irrelevant; at market open on a central-bank announcement day it may be unacceptable.

Input and output drift

Models are trained and evaluated on historical distributions of inputs and outputs. In production, these distributions can change:

- The mix of languages, sectors, or sources in the news feed may shift.
- Corporate communication style may evolve (e.g., more ESG language).
- Market microstructure characteristics (volatility, liquidity) may change.

Drift monitoring tracks:

- summary statistics of inputs (e.g., document length, sentiment lexicon counts, sector coverage);
- the distribution of LLM outputs (scores, classifications, confidence measures);
- the relationship between outputs and realized returns (e.g., rolling information coefficients).

When monitored carefully, these signals can trigger alerts such as "LLM scores for financials have become much more concentrated near zero" or "the correlation between sentiment and next-week returns has halved over the last quarter."

Business KPIs and guardrails

Ultimately, monitoring must connect back to what matters for the business:

- hit rates and risk-adjusted returns of LLM-driven trades versus benchmarks;

- realized turnover and transaction costs compared with expectations;
- contribution to overall portfolio risk factors and drawdowns.

Guardrails can be implemented as automated checks on these KPIs, for example:

- If the rolling one-month Sharpe ratio of the LLM sleeve falls below a threshold, automatically reduce its maximum allowed risk budget or notify the strategy owner.
- If realized turnover exceeds a pre-agreed cap for several days, throttle order sizes or investigate input volatility.
- If the strategy's exposure to a specific sector or factor breaches limits due to correlated LLM recommendations, route decisions through additional human review.

These mechanisms ensure that the LLM's influence on the portfolio scales up and down smoothly with its observed performance and stability.

Human-in-the-Loop and Control Workflows

Even with sophisticated automation, human oversight remains essential, especially during early deployment or for strategies with large capital at risk.

Approval and override patterns

Common interaction patterns between humans and LLM systems include:

- **Pre-trade approval.** The system proposes trades, and a human must explicitly approve, modify, or reject them before execution. This is typical when first rolling out a new LLM-driven signal.

- **Soft overrides.** The system executes trades automatically within specified bounds, but traders can adjust or cancel orders when they disagree with the LLM's rationale.
- **Post-trade review.** Risk or compliance teams review a sample of LLM-influenced trades, including prompts and responses, to verify that they align with policy and that rationales are sensible.

Such workflows should be designed to scale: interfaces must surface the most relevant information (e.g., summary rationales, key documents, confidence scores) without overwhelming the reviewer.

Explanation and documentation at decision time

For model risk and regulatory reasons, it is increasingly important to provide *explanations* at the time decisions are made. LLMs are well suited to this, but explanations must be constrained and logged.

Good practice includes:

- generating short, structured rationales alongside each recommendation (e.g., "positive revenue surprise," "improved guidance," "valuation still below sector peers");
- linking each rationale to underlying documents and timestamps so that reviewers can reconstruct the chain of evidence;
- avoiding free-form, speculative narratives in the production path that could confuse or mislead human overseers.

These explanations help humans understand when to trust or challenge the model and create an auditable record of why certain decisions were made.

Compliance, Model Risk, and Auditability

Regulated institutions must treat LLM-based components as part of their model inventory. That means aligning with internal model risk management (MRM) frameworks and external regulations.

Sensitive data and privacy

LLM prompts may include:

- proprietary trading positions and orders;
- client-specific information;
- non-public research or risk views.

To avoid leaks and privacy violations:

- apply redaction or tokenization to personally identifiable or client-identifying information before it enters the LLM;
- restrict which models and third-party providers can see sensitive prompts (on-premises or virtual private deployments may be required for highly confidential data);
- segregate logs so that sensitive content is stored securely, with access controls and retention policies consistent with legal requirements.

These measures should be documented and reviewed regularly by data-protection and compliance teams.

Model risk management lifecycle

Within a typical MRM framework, each material LLM component should have:

- a clearly defined purpose and scope (what decisions it supports, what it does *not* do);
- documented data lineage and preprocessing steps;
- documented training, calibration, and backtesting procedures, including controls against leakage and overfitting as discussed in previous sections;
- defined performance thresholds and monitoring plans;
- change-control processes for any updates to model, prompts, or surrounding logic.

Independent validation functions should be able to reproduce key results and verify that implementation matches documentation. For LLMs, this includes verifying that prompts and retrieval configurations in production match those used in approved backtests, or that any differences were properly authorized and re-tested.

Experiment tracking and lineage

Because LLM systems evolve rapidly—new model versions, prompt tweaks, added tools—an explicit experiment and configuration tracking system is essential. At minimum, you should be able to answer:

- Which model (and version) produced this particular recommendation?
- What prompt template and configuration (retrieval depth, context window, sampling settings) were used?
- Which data sources and document versions fed into the decision?
- Which code and infrastructure versions were in place at the time?

Pragmatically, this is often implemented via:

- version control for code and prompt templates;
- a configuration store for model and deployment parameters;
- an experiment-tracking system that records data snapshots, metric results, and derived artifacts for each major backtest or offline evaluation;
- structured logging in production that tags every request and response with the relevant version identifiers.

Having this lineage not only supports post-mortems and audits; it also accelerates research by making it clear which variants have been tried and how they performed.

Bringing It All Together

A production-grade LLM trading stack is more than a model API bolted onto a trading system. It is a carefully orchestrated ensemble of:

- data ingestion and preprocessing pipelines that respect event time and information sets;
- serving architectures that match latency needs and provide clear SLOs and fallbacks;
- monitoring layers that track technical health, statistical drift, and business performance;
- human-in-the-loop workflows that allow for oversight and intervention; and
- governance, compliance, and lineage mechanisms that make the entire system auditable and accountable.

When these elements are aligned with the evaluation and risk disciplines developed earlier in the chapter, the "autonomous analyst" becomes a reliable member of the trading team: not infallible, but understandable, controllable, and improvable over time.

www.ingramcontent.com/pod-product-compliance
Lightning Source LLC
LaVergne TN
LVHW022157200926
848481LV00006B/1772
* 9 7 9 8 8 9 6 6 5 2 3 5 9 *